Praise For The Cruelest Con

"By their very nature adoption experiences are emotionally charged and can provide the highest highs or the lowest of lows. In *The Cruelest Con,* Kelly Kiser-Mostrom shares personal and invaluable information: a necessary reading for the protection of children, birth parents, and adoptive parents."—**Jane E. Ryan**, author of *Broken Spirits ~ Lost Souls: Loving Children with Attachment and Bonding Difficulties.*

"This is a poignant story of the painful journey of one family, as the result of an adoption scam/fraud. Scams prey on the hopes and dreams of prospective parents. While the vast majority of adoptions do not involve fraud, this book is important reading for prospective adoptive parents so they will become educated consumers."—**Kathleen Silber, MSW, ACSW**. Co-author *Dear Birthmother* and *Children of Open Adoption*

"It has long been recognized that couples seeking to adopt children often feel particularly vulnerable. After years of unsuccessful medical treatments and finally the acceptance of infertility, the quest to find a child or children is still difficult and the road full of detours and pitfalls. Add to this the experience of Kelly Kiser-Mostrom and her husband being defrauded and exploited and you have a nightmare of huge proportions. The Cruelest Con outlines over two years of their life, being bilked, manipulated and lied to by a master criminal, Sonya Furlow, posing as an adoption facilitator. Along with the Mostroms, dozens of other couples lost hundreds of thousands of dollars and were deprived of their fondest dreams over and over again. This is an important book for those considering adoption to read and to integrate. There may not be many Furlows lurking out there, but it only takes one to create incredible havoc."—**Annette Baran, MSW, LCSW**, co-author of *Adoption Triangle* and *Lethal Secrets*

The Cruelest Con

The Cruelest Con

✦

The Guide for a S.a.F.E. Adoption Journey

Kelly Kiser-Mostrom

iUniverse, Inc.

New York Lincoln Shanghai

The Cruelest Con
The Guide for a S.a.F.E. Adoption Journey

Copyright © 2005 by Kelly Kiser-Mostrom

iUniverse books may be ordered through booksellers or by contacting:

iUniverse
2021 Pine Lake Road, Suite 100
Lincoln, NE 68512
www.iuniverse.com
1-800-Authors (1-800-288-4677)

ISBN-13: 978-0-595-34998-2 (pbk)
ISBN-13: 978-0-595-79708-0 (ebk)
ISBN-10: 0-595-34998-6 (pbk)
ISBN-10: 0-595-79708-3 (ebk)

Printed in the United States of America

Contents

Acknowledgments

Throughout this journey this book would not be possible without the guidance, encouragement and support of some fabulous people. There are not enough words to say just how much I appreciate them and their spirit!

To my husband, Ken, thank you for having the faith, patience and understanding. You are my soul mate and I will love you forever.

To my children, thank you for being you and understanding how important this project was to mom. You are all special blessings! I love you all always!

To Ellen, Jane and Maria, thank you for sharing your knowledge, support and keeping me on the right path. Though you had to redirect me many times without the three of you this book would not be a reality. Thanks for sticking by me, keeping me focused and reminding me to look forward.

To my Internet buddy, Kelly, thank you for being by me through the years, for understanding when no one else could, for calming my fears and for all your support. Even when you were at your lowest you were there for me and accepted me for me! Big thanks to you and Steve for allowing me to share parts of your life throughout this book.

To Dad and Mom, Jon and Phyllis, Belinda, Kim, Beth and Kathy, thank you for listening and for trying so desperately to understand our situation and have empathy.

To all those I interviewed, thank you for sharing your stories, thoughts and feelings with so much compassion and understanding.

To Sonya Furlow's victims, thank you for having the courage to stand up and help uncover her scam, and for all of your support when you too were all hurting so desperately. I hope the world has been a little kinder and gentler to you all.

To all of the readers, thank you for reading this book and keeping in mind that adoption can truly be a wonderful journey. It is a work from my heart not written to discourage you but to help protect you, give you hope and to put things in perspective.

Foreword

By Ellen Roseman

In the course of facilitating open adoptions for the last 25 years, I have seen and experienced numerous changes with the practice of adoption. When my husband and I adopted two baby girls ten weeks apart in 1980, the adoptions were closed. At the time, that seemed appropriate to us. When the girls were infants I attended a lecture presented by agency social worker and author Sharon Kaplan Roszia about adoption changes needing to be made based on her decades of work in the field. This eloquent and gracious speaker was mesmerizing to me as she talked about her "adoption mistakes coming back to haunt her including scams." After hearing Sharon speak, I knew I had to try to open up the girls' adoptions and integrate their birth families into our lives. It took time and energy, but eventually we were all able to come together so the girls would have genetic continuity. Almost twenty-five years later, these open adoptions are pretty much a big "ho hum" in our family.

My husband and I "wandered" into adoption without benefit of adoption knowledge or education. He was a physician who relinquished a baby boy to a closed adoption when in college. I had not only been adopted in a stepparent adoption, but was raising a foster child, still; we knew little about loss and child welfare issues. In looking back I think we were fortunate not to become involved in an adoption scam.

In 1980, there were few books to read about adoption. I read "The Adoption Triangle" written by eminent social workers Annette Baran and Reuben Pannor, which presented longitudinal studies on adoptees in the closed system. It made a strong recommendation for opening up adoptions. These remarkable clinicians as directors of a well-known agency in Los Angeles had come to the same conclusion as Sharon and others: it was time to have openness between adoptive parents and birth families. Records were never sealed to keep the two sides apart, but because of the strong "stigma" experienced by an adoptee whose birth certificate routinely would be stamped "illegitimate" when the parents were not married. Sealing records solved this problem and provided privacy for the adoptee. Still, I was seeing nothing in print about preventing adoption scamming. Books were being written on the "psychology of the adoptive child," "Attachment," "Infertility," "How to adopt," "Open Adoption," and much more, but there was virtually nothing in writing about adoption scams which could be useful and educational.

All during the 1980's, as someone who facilitated open adoptions, I would occasionally hear stories about adoption scams. The news media seemed to focus on prospective birth parents trying to sell a baby, but just as often I was reading about dishonest lawyers, agencies, and facilitators. Occasionally, there were even stories about questionable adoptive parents. The most vivid case was the "Lisa" story out of New York who was murdered by her adoptive father when she was five. Unknown to her birth mother at placement time, a legal adoption never took place.

When I lived in Arizona one agency, which upped its fee from $25,000 to $30,000, for a placement in the 1980's went bankrupt leaving its clients without either their funds or a baby as planned. Scams are not something new in adoption. Well-documented stories exist about the "Tennessee Children's Home Society" under the direction of Georgia Tann. Her stealing of babies and toddlers from families during the years 1924-1949 with the help of a well-known judge made headlines. Her death prevented her prosecution, which was imminent. A well-known television film about her life, which starred Mary Tyler Moore, can still be seen on occasion. It is chilling and shocking to see that this was done under the guise of decency and respectability. Tennessee was one of the early states to mandate opening records to adoptees partially because of this horrific history.

Another agency faced an indictment for unethical practices: the newspapers reported Arizona was the ninth state to indict this Illinois based agency. This agency is still licensed and operating in several states doing what I call "legalized baby selling." I have learned there are always families willing to pay almost anything for a baby, which is why these unscrupulous agencies are able to still be in business. Not only agencies can be outright dishonest, but also lawyers and facilitators have their share of news making headlines. Even Christian based adoption organizations have had their share of newsworthy stories. In a business in which the rare commodity is a healthy child, dishonesty takes place on occasion when money exchanges hands in large amounts. It is easy as an adoption practitioner to feel one is doing "God's work," and lose sight of who the client really is....not the people paying or earning the money, but the innocent precious child.

Not only were social work standards changing, but also the Internet was bringing massive changes. Searches and reunions could be completed with the help of the Internet. Programs such as "Unsolved Mysteries" were presenting people looking to "find and connect." Adoptive couples were beginning to advertise not only in newspapers, but also on the Internet and adoption professionals found they were able to build expansive websites in order to advertise services. Anyone could do this whether qualified or not. And, adoptees were lobbying to have their records unsealed citing their right to have pertinent information about themselves. Many adoptees believe it is a civil rights issue to have this access. Each time a state opens records providing the original birth certificate, etc. it has been found birth parents overwhelmingly support these changes.

RESOLVE, which is a national organization designed to help infertile couples make helpful choices about family building was helpful in areas in which there were chapters, but in many states pre-adoptive couples did not have this kind of resource available to them to help learn and sort out the many available options. People could choose from agency or independent adoption, closed or open, domestic or international, and even newborn or older child adoptions, throw in the Indian Child Welfare Act which applies if a child is part Native American and you have another set of complex laws to observe, then, you have the "birth father" who is often missing and the many laws governing his rights. Terrifying stories such as "Baby Jessica" in which she was returned because her birth father opposed adoption would make anyone hesitant to adopt. With much media focusing on horror stories a prudent question to ask: "Is adoption worth the risks financially and emotionally?" The answer is definitely "yes."

Over time, I began to see there was a crucial need for "education" provided to pre-adoptive parents and birth parents about this complex and often confusing process. I slowly began building an educational program as a way to "inoculate" and "protect" people from scams. I saw that pre-adoptive couples were extremely vulnerable because of their desire to have a child and that without good solid professional guidance, scamming was a likelihood. Over the years I developed "do's and don'ts" for my clients such as "If is seems too good to be true, it probably is." "Or, if a large sum of money is involved, beware." The best one is "if a professional indicates they have many birth moms-sort of a candy store, be cautious." Often when I tell a pre-adoptive couple that calls me, that I have what I call a "working service" full of assignments, I sometimes hear: "Don't you just have a waiting list of babies you give out? We don't have time to do assignments and learn." I wonder what these people think about the time it takes to raise a child?

Probably the saddest calls I receive are those from couples or singles who have been scammed monetarily and emotionally while trying to adopt. The voice at the other end of the call is always in shock trying to figure out how to cope and go forth. For as long as I have received these calls, my heart always goes out to the family calling. With the media focusing on the "dark side" of adoption, there is a tendency to think that scams are an every day occurrence. Yet, as someone who works hard to educate and protect prospective adoptive parents and birth families, I can tell you from my viewpoint it is rare. Knowledge is power…and education in depth helps to eliminate fear.

When Kelly first called and began sharing her horrific and tangled story, I found her saga to be fascinating and compelling. My mind raced as I took copious notes. I knew right away she needed to take some "strong action steps" which would help with healing even if the so-called adoption provider was not prosecuted. Most likely, she and Ken would recover no money, but, at least, they could feel empowered by doing everything possible so that no one else would be victimized in the same way. They needed to do something about the feelings of "betrayal" and being "victimized."

Kelly was open to my suggestions as we began exploring possibilities. I told her not to be discouraged when hearing a "no, not interested" and to "persist." First calls to the FBI are generally ignored. The same is true when calling news programs such as 20/20, 60 minutes, 48 Hours, or Dateline. Information posted on the Internet did produce other families also scammed and that bolstered Kelly's confidence as well as her depleted energy. She and Ken were not alone. Her instincts were right on. I was sure a scam was involved from her story and she was sure.

I admired Kelly's ability to persevere and stay on task during this difficult and stressful time. Day by day and week by week her journey began to take shape as she pursued all options presented. She stayed in touch with other couples encouraging them to follow through and stay informed. And, throughout all of this we still found moments to talk about her dreams of family building through adoption: she did not lose sight of her ultimate goal…. to add a child or children to her family.

Once the trial concluded, I provided Kelly the information needed to contact the bonding company who held the bond for her California facilitator. This facilitator did what I refer to as "piggybacking" onto another facilitator's services in Pennsylvania. This is where one practitioner charges a fee, then puts the client in touch with another adoption practitioner who then charges yet another fee. In California, by law, all facilitators have to carry a $10,000 bond. I knew the California facilitator was bonded and liable for what she did. When a wonderful gift from "Omaha Steaks" arrived on my doorstep shortly thereafter, I knew Kelly and Ken had been successful in recouping some of the monies lost when hiring unethical so called "adoption facilitators." I was thrilled for them with yet another victory in this long journey back to emotional and financial healing. As an adoption facilitator, I was glad to give something back.

Finally, I encouraged Kelly to write a book about this experience into the dark side of adoption. I believed it would greatly help others. I knew as someone who often reviews adoption related books for various publications, there was no comprehensive up-to-date overview about adoption scamming. Kelly's book admirably and completely fills this much-needed large gap.

The reader will be horrified and fascinated by this story. In it she gives critical and thoughtful insights into the turbulent waters faced when dealing with agencies, lawyers, and facilitators. "*The Cruelest Con*" is an indispensable resource for anyone thinking about adopting a child. Her book makes a prudent plea to thoroughly research when hiring any adoption professional in any part of the country. I think an underlying message in her story is about the importance of open adoption in this new millennium. Because all involved are known to one another in open adoption, there is less of a chance of being scammed by an unscrupulous so-called professional.

Also, according to Child Welfare League of America longitudinal studies, it is in the "best interest of the child" to provide genetic continuity with birth family being involved in the child's life long term. True, this can be frightening to most people, but education can and will build confidence taking people out of fear and mythology into what is true and real in adoption. Some adoption professionals believe it best not to have their clients read or see scary stories such as Kelly's. It is my goal the readers see this book as a "tool" to help enhance and help in the adoption experience.

Each chapter written in Kelly's engaging and eloquent personal voice is must read for anyone thinking about the adoption process. It is a story about resilience, determination, and most of all healing. It is a courageous journey in which justice triumphed as one family continues to try to make a difference for so many others. It has been a privilege for me to be a part of Kelly and Ken's healing journey and I believe the reader will also feel the power of her positive message just as I have.

Prologue

The Cruelest Con is the mesmerizing, and heartbreaking true story of an adoptive parents journey across country in an attempt to complete their family. An inside look into one of the nation's largest, precedent setting adoption schemes. It reveals the deception, manipulation, ecstasy, love and understanding that lead you on an emotional roller coaster ride. *The Cruelest Con* reveals how the FBI and a multitude of others joined forces to bring to a halt one woman's treacherous schemes that shattered the dreams of over 44 adoptive parents. This book heightens your awareness on the loving gift of adoption while revealing telltale-warning signs in the pursuit of the adoption dream. *The Cruelest Con* is the chilling echo of a judge's words that will captivate your heart.

The Cruelest Con is a personal story of how a family was caught in the middle of a nationwide adoption scam. As one of Sonya's victims said at her sentencing, I need to "make lemonade out of lemons." That is the purpose of this book. As you read *The Cruelest Con* you will find other scams that have devastated other peoples lives all across this nation. Throughout the book you will discover a vast array of resources that will help lead you down the path of a positive adoption journey. Adoption is and will always be an emotional journey for all members of the triad. Often the lack of control and unknown can disrupt the lives of many. If God forbid you are exposed to or suffer a "loss" in an adoption scam this can be a traumatic and long lasting effect on a persons life. Like others who experience major life losses often times facing such a horrendous situation results in them experiencing depression, posttraumatic stress syndrome, guilt, grief, and a gamut of other strong emotions whose eruption makes ordinary everyday life difficult. This book was written in hopes that it will empower, educate, and help protect you.

The Internet has changed the adoption world. It provides a vast amount of resources yet at the same time, it opens the door to unscrupulous people looking to prey on others emotions to make a fast buck. With the introduction of the Internet, adoption scams have become more prevalent and have left people devastated and unsure of where to turn to when seeking recourse or justice. This book is meant to help avoid such situations. The dark side of the adoption world needs to be put in perspective. Thousands of wonderful adoption experiences happen

1

every year. Even though scams are increasing you can have that wonderful experience by educating yourself, and thoroughly researching your options.

Best wishes on your safe and happy adoption journey!

Introduction

I was driving home from work at 4:15 p.m. on Halloween of 1990. It was a beautiful day, the sun was shining and it was unusually warm for that time of year. As I was driving down our gravel road my mind began to wander. All of a sudden it dawned on me that I had not thought about our pending adoption for quite some time. After five years of infertility treatments we had been waiting since August of 1988 for the arrival of our child through adoption. I reassured myself that someday our long wait would be over. But life was good for us. We were finally getting settled after moving to a new town five months earlier. As I approached the stop sign close to our home all thoughts disappeared. I could see the neighbor children all dressed up for Halloween and standing at my front door.

As I turned into our driveway they ran and hid behind the large bush near our front door. I pretended I hadn't seen them and chuckled to myself as I pulled into the garage. Moments after entering the house the doorbell rang. I was struggling to keep a straight face when I tried to guess who was behind those masks. After a short conversation they ran home giggling at their silly neighbor who didn't see them hiding behind the bush.

I went to change out of my suit and was half dressed as the phone rang. The voice on the other end said, "Hi Kelly, how are you?" I don't remember what my reply was. I just kept thinking I know this voice but for the life of me I couldn't figure out who it was. He proceeded to ask about my husband and work. Then finally he said "Are you ready to be parents?" I sunk to my knees and tears streamed down my face. For at that moment I knew it was the Executive Director from our adoption agency. He told me we were proud parents of a baby girl and we could pick her up the next day at five o'clock. All thoughts vanished from my mind. He was so pleasantly comforting and wanted to make sure I was in the right frame of mind to drive to Ken's place of employment to tell him the exciting news.

This awesome news had to be told in person. I had to come up with an excuse to get Ken to come home or meet me at his job in private. I quickly called Ken and said "You have got to come home and see what we got in the mail today!" Of course he was busy and didn't know if he would be able to break away. Then he began to insist that I tell him what it was. I told him he had to see for himself and to meet me in the parking lot at his work. I frantically ran to our bedroom and finished dressing. I got in the car and raced to his company parking lot. After waiting for five minutes, which seemed like an hour, I gave up and walked up to the shop doors. Our friend and his co-worker was the first to see me. By the look on his face he knew something was wrong. Of course, who wouldn't? I was standing there with tears and mascara streaming down my cheeks and two different shoes on. With a panicked look on his face my husband came out quickly and asked what was wrong. It wasn't until later that I found out my husband and his co-worker had thought someone had died. But on the contrary there was a new life, our beautiful daughter! Oh, what a great holiday Halloween was!

Now as I look back time has gone so quickly, she is growing up before my eyes. Her favorite bedtime story was about that wonderful day and the next day when we first laid eyes on our beautiful daughter and met her birth parents. They were so young, yet so mature and unselfish. In our happiness there was also sorrow to see how much pain and grieving they were experiencing. Our daughter knows that they loved her very much but were unable to give her the life they wanted her to have. For them and for our daughter we thank the Lord above for leading us along the path of adoption. We know now we were much better parents for having to wait so long. Our daughter was worth the wait!

May the Lord always keep her in the palm of His hand!

PART I
The Journey

1

The Hook

Wednesday, August 26, 1998, after years and months of waiting for a second child Kloe Martis had finally arrived. She was born into this confusing world by C-section, weighing 6 pounds, 12 ounces and was 18 ½ inches long. Kloe was born in Philadelphia, Pennsylvania, hundreds and hundreds of miles away from us. Soon she would meet her adoptive parent's and travel across country to a small town in Nebraska. My heart ached to hold her, to touch the softness of her skin, to watch every breath she took. My husband, Ken and I wondered whether she had fuzzy light brown or dark hair, pink or golden cheeks. Were Kloe and her birth mother, Deena getting the best possible care the hospital could offer? Our minds were racing with excitement and frustration. Then reality finally reared its ugly head. It was possible that Kloe was not going to be a part of our family. All the months of prayers, worrying, waiting and wondering would soon come to an end.

Sonya Furlow, the adoption facilitator and owner of Tender Hearts Family Services, left a message on our voice mail that we needed to call her as soon as possible. As we listened further there was a second message from Sonya. Frantically, I made dozens of attempts to call her, my stomach was in knots, and I couldn't breathe, or concentrate. I was terrified Deena was having second thoughts about continuing with the adoption plan. Thoughts were racing through my mind. Was Royce, the birth father, with her? How was he feeling? Where were Deena's other children? Was everyone as emotionally exhausted as we were? Finally by the middle of the day and with my anxiety level at an all time high, Sonya answered her phone.

"Sonya this is Kelly, I got your message to call. What's going on? I am going crazy just sitting and wondering what is happening."

With the tone of disgust, Sonya said, "Hi Kelly. Well Deena wants the baby to go to cradle care, before she signs the relinquishments."

"She wants to see how her other children will deal with the adoption before she actually places the baby with you. Also, Royce is back in town. He is with Deena at this moment, but they are not communicating." She stated matter of fact.

"Meaning what? I asked.

"Deena isn't speaking to Royce because he hasn't been in her life since she made the adoption plan. Royce, on the other hand thought that was what Deena wanted." She replied.

Tears began to well up in my eyes, and I asked, "So what in the world do we do now?"

"We will just have to wait and see if Deena signs the relinquishment papers after her 72 hours are up. If she doesn't and she is still uncertain, the baby will go into foster care." She said with no emotion.

"Oh, Sonya, for how long?" I queried.

"Who knows Kelly, it could be two weeks, three months or longer. If she signs after the 72 hours, according to Pennsylvania laws, you will still have 40 days where she can change her mind." Sonya stated.

"Forty days! We cannot continue to be on this emotional roller coaster ride for that long. What happens after the 40 days?" I asked.

"At that point Kelly, your attorney Jay Ginsburg can request a court date here in Philly for the termination of rights and then it could take another 20 to 30 days to get on the court docket. Although one thing you need to know is that according to Pennsylvania laws, you and Ken will be responsible for paying the cradle care cost, because this is a private placement." She said.

"How much does that cost? And is cradle care the same as foster care?" I questioned.

Sonya replied, "Yes, cradle care and foster care are the same thing. It will run you about $40.00 to $65.00 a day."

"Sonya, I don't know if we can afford that! We only budgeted so much money for this adoption," I stated frantically.

"Well my mom does foster care for me once in a while, but she has not being feeling well and she is already taking care of one child for me. I do have a wonderful family that adopted from me about a year ago that would maybe do the cradle care for me as a favor. You know they are wanting to adopt again here in the next few months," Sonya replied.

"So Kloe could be almost three months old before we would be able to bring her home?" I asked feeling deflated.

"Yes, Kelly, I am afraid so." Sonya stated.

"This just makes me sick to my stomach to think that Kloe will spend the first few months of her life in foster care. What about the important first months of bonding? I can't bear to think she will be all alone in foster care with strangers." I replied with uncontrollable tears streaming down my face.

"Sonya what are we suppose to do?" I asked.

"Sit tight. I will go back to see Deena tomorrow and lets just wait and see what happens. Maybe after she sees the baby she will come to some resolution. Send me some more of your profiles and I'll start circulating them to some of my other birth mothers that are not matched yet. Then I'll call you tomorrow," she replied.

"Alright, please call as soon as you can." I stated.

"I am sorry Kelly, I will try my best to get Deena to see what is best for this baby. She just cannot afford another child, but I have to be careful when I talk to her. If not the adoption could be overturned if the court thinks I coerced her in anyway," Sonya said.

"I understand it has to be Deena's decision. I don't want you to do anything that would jeopardize the adoption. It must be her decision. She has to be going through a very difficult time. Tell her our thoughts and prayers are with her and we are here if she wants to talk. This has to be the most important decision she has ever made in her life and we only want what is best for her and her baby," I replied.

"I will let Deena know I spoke with you. Kelly, make sure you and Ken take care and try to get some sleep tonight. I know God has a baby for you," Sonya said sympathetically.

The receiver clicked and slowly I set the phone down. My tears would not stop. I felt as though I had to vomit. All I could think of was all these months of sitting by the phone, changing some of our life plans, checking my email five or more times a day and hoping and praying for this baby, and suddenly it was about to come to an end. Since the end of July, Deena had been ordered to bed rest by her physician because of some threatening health problems related to complications with pre-eclampsyia. Our thoughts or at least hopes were she would have a clearer picture of whether to proceed with the adoption or not.

As I slouched in an overstuffed loveseat I wondered how in the world was I going to explain this to our daughter, Kassie. Our first beautiful baby was growing up so fast, but no second grader needed to bear this type of disappointment. I was afraid this might be too much for an eight year old to comprehend. We wanted so much for her to feel a part of this adoption, so Kassie would know how special adoption is and what a wonderful experience it was when she was adopted. Thoughts of that wonderful fall day, with the excitement and happiness we felt when we got "the call", began to revolve in my mind. Tears began streaming down my face, tears of happiness and overwhelming joy! After five years of infertility treatments and waiting our dreams had finally come true. We were parents of a beautiful daughter through the loving gift of adoption. For the last two years at dinner and at bedtime she always prayed, "Dear God, thank you for this wonderful day and please let us get a baby. Amen." I knew Kassie would be devastated if Deena changed her mind and decided to parent her child.

How did this happen? I kept repeating to myself, "God does not give us what we cannot handle." Trying to convince myself that everything would be all right. Only a few months ago I felt so confident and excited in our decision to use a facilitator. We knew the risk. So I thought. One thing was for sure; I did not fully consider the emotional risks.

◆   ◆   ◆

It all began in January 1998, Kay, our caseworker, from a Nebraska agency called.

"It is time for your home study update." She said.

Kay had been our caseworker for almost eight years; she was a lovely, kind and compassionate woman who was always available at a moment's notice. Kay was going to be retiring the following May and I was really hoping we would have completed our family before she retired. Upon her arrival for the routine visit we discussed the standard grueling protocol. It was time for new medical physicals and submitting a statement of financial condition. Papers were signed to allow the agency to run our names through the criminal history and child abuse registries. Once that paperwork was completed then it was time to review the checklist of what type of child we were looking to adopt. I despised this part of the home study. Remembering vividly the first time we had to do this I felt like I was walking through the yellow pages or shopping in a catalog. It was a strange and uncomfortable feeling. In retrospect, I now know that is not at all the case. Adoptive parents must know their limitations. We decided it was time to be more open and accept an older child or small sibling group. We just wanted to be parents one more time.

Enthusiastically, I asked Kay, "What can we do to be more proactive? We are really getting impatient and this waiting is so hard. It's especially difficult when you want something so bad that should be just a normal part of life and yet you have no control over the outcome." Kay suggested we network and provided us with the name of another Nebraska couple that found their child through an email Christian adoption list.

After Kay left, I felt renewed and once again hopeful and excited. What a great idea! We had just purchased a new computer and it never dawned on us to research and network over the Internet. Within a matter of weeks I was hooked! I began joining several email lists, visited adoption web sites and became totally enthralled with the vast amount of information available. I was a little leery or maybe paranoid at that point. You really don't know with whom you are corresponding with or who is reading your information. I slowly began to test the waters by posting anonymously to web sites asking for information and not leaving my email address.

Several months passed. Every waking moment, from the first thing in the morning till the wee hours of the night I watched the Internet bulletin boards absorbing any and all information I could find. Finally we jumped in and wrote a "Dear Birth Parent" letter. Adoption.com hosted our letter and pictures for a small fee and we set up an email box to correspond with prospective birth mothers. Basically we were marketing ourselves and this was a new concept to us. It made me feel vulnerable and awkward to have so much information out there for the world to see. I felt like I had been living in a box, the vast amount of websites, resources and support groups were all so amazing and overwhelming.

Up to this point I never knew what a "bulletin board" was. It was all so simple. You write a question or message and wait for others to write a reply. Anyone who has access to the Internet would be able to see what you write. Upon reading these boards I discovered discussion threads about adoption facilitators. Having never heard of an adoption facilitator that became my new main focus. They certainly seemed to complete adoptions faster then the traditional agencies. I quickly discovered that most people were either pro facilitator or totally against them. There were risks but I had to find out more. Little could I anticipate the torturous journey that was about to begin.

From all the information I found, the only thing facilitators did was match prospective adoptive parents with a prospective birth mother, for a matching fee. Where it was legal many lawyers and agencies had a facilitator or two working for them as well. Facilitators are not licensed, nor are they regulated. I learned the process was risky because the match could fall through, although most facilitators would roll your money over into another situation. If living expenses had been paid to the birth mother you could lose that money. We didn't have to worry about living expenses because paying for most of those expenses was illegal in Nebraska. In the state of California there seemed to be more facilitators then in the rest of the country. I assumed that was why the state of California required facilitators to be bonded in the amount of $10,000, which was just about the amount we could spend. I found some comfort in knowing about the bonding information and really felt that was a positive safety net put in place to protect the adoptive parents. A bond was insurance that was purchased by the facilitator in the event of fraud or other mishandled circumstances.

It was just amazing to me that all the laws in each state were different. You have to check each state's laws so you do not get caught in something illegal that would jeopardize an adoption. Since facilitators are not licensed or regulated, the only way you can check them out is to call the Better Business Bureau and the state's Attorney General. Then you could follow up by calling references, checking posts on the Internet and talking to anyone you could who had previously worked with a particular facilitator. Unfortunately, during the early stages of my research I did not discover that there was a difference in facilitators or realize that a few facilitators provided educational services. Later I learned that some are "working facilitators" who provide educational services and help teach you how to network. Other facilitators are "piggybacking facilitators" who find prospective birth mothers through agencies, attorneys or other facilitators. When this happens you are not paying just one facilitator fee but the fees of two adoption professionals, the facilitator you signed on with and the adoption professional who the prospective birth mother is working with. It is crucial that you understand the difference between the types of facilitators.

One thing that intrigued me about using the facilitators was many of their web sites listed actual prospective birth mothers in search of adoptive parents. Oddly enough, I had always thought there was one healthy infant available for adoption to sixty adoptive couples. Each of these listings included the prospective birth mothers' age, a brief history and total costs involved. Wow! I thought. "Have I been living in a box or what? Look at how easy this looks and most facilitators tout their placement rate at 6 to 8 months, upon signing with them." Adoption Visions out of Berkeley, California, was the first to catch my eye. Their application fee was only a $100 and an additional $2000 was required upon the acceptance of a match with a prospective birth mother. After researching several other specific facilitator's I determined their prices ranged from $3000 to $6800, for the same services. I remembered seeing a couple of web sites where other members of the adoption triad were warning others not to pay upfront fees. So certainly Adoption Visions policy was to our advantage. Adoption Visions had an email list we subscribed to, which told brief histories about the available children or the prospective birth mother. When I saw the first list, I was shocked and enthused. The list was amazing and gave me instant hope that our family would some day be completed! Some of the adoptions costs started at $8500 and went all the way up to $25,000. My adrenaline started pumping every time I received this list, and before I knew it I was hooked. This list became my lifeline. It wouldn't be until many months later that I would begin to refer to these lists as "bait and switch". A method to entice clients into a service, only to find out all or the majority of the prospective birth mothers had already been matched.

We were also getting some hits on our profile at adoption.com. Only three of these contacts actually turned out to be legitimate prospective birth parents; the others were scams. It became my mission each day to race home from work on my break and lunch hour to check my email and scope out the boards for any possible leads. After all, the quicker you were to respond the better off you were. Right?

We were aware that agencies in Nebraska and the Midwest generally charged around $10,000 to $12,000 for an adoption and some of Adoption Visions fees were reasonable; an amount most people pay for a new car. I knew that comparison was awful and struck a cord with me. It was one that I had saw posted many times on the bulletin boards. An adoption should have no monetary cost, no one can buy an individual and no price should ever be placed on life. I had to convince myself to look at the adoption as though we were paying for the facilitator's time and efforts in coordinating the adoption. We were also aware that on the east coast and in other parts of the country agency fees could be as high as $45,000 or more. Regardless of the amount, there was one problem; we didn't have that kind of money.

In researching our options I found that some sites offered bank loans for adoptions. Then a few bulletin boards with creative adoptive moms explained how they would conduct fundraisers. Bingo! I had an idea! Thinking out loud I said, "Why didn't I think of this a long time ago, I am a banker?" Interest rates were at an all time low and we had a 30-year mortgage on our home at a fixed rate of 9%. We could refinance our home to get a lower rate, tack on a little extra for siding for the house, and add enough to the loan based on the average adoption costs.

Ken and I discussed the refinancing and decided it was time to do something. Both of us were close to 40 years old. We had started our first adoption journey in the late 1980's and at that time a couple of agencies in Nebraska would not consider applications from prospective adoptive parents over forty. With this memory lingering in the back of our minds we also discussed wanting to get our children through college before we retired and still be young enough to enjoy our grandchildren. I spoke with my co-worker at the bank and she agreed to refinance our home at 6.5% and add enough on to the loan for the adoption. Everything seemed to be falling into place.

I was very enthusiastic when Ken got home from work. We went out to dinner with close friends and discussed my research on facilitators and Adoption Visions. Our friends were excited and full of encouragement. Ken was skeptical which was out of character for him.

"Kel, that is a lot of money. Maybe we should just be thankful for being able to parent one child. I know you really want this. Are you sure Adoption Visions is legit?" He stated.

I replied, "As far as I can see. I am very thankful for Kassie; she has been a joy from the moment she was born. I feel we have more love to give and you are such a great dad. Also, Kassie is just dying to have a sister or brother. I want her to have life long sibling relationships."

We spent several hours discussing all the information I'd collected from the Better Business Bureau, the references I had called, posts on the Internet and specific web sites that revealed warnings about specific adoption professionals and scams. Adoption Visions came up with a clean slate. By the time we were pulling into the driveway, we had arrived with a consensus. "Let's go for it!" Ken said enthused. That night I had a terrible time sleeping. I couldn't seem to think about anything other than Adoption Visions and what was to come in the following months. Too restless to sleep, I quietly crawled out of bed and went to the basement to surf the Net.

The next morning, I filled out the lengthy application that I had received by email from Adoption Visions. The application seemed unprofessional, there were several typos and only a small amount of space was provided for us to complete our answers to the questions. I hated filling out adoption applications. Each time I completed an application it was like baring your whole life story and soul to a total stranger. I knew these people knew more about us as a couple then most of our own family members. The next thing on my agenda was to call Kay at our adoption agency. She was as usual very helpful in explaining how the agency could help us and was confident they would support or help us in any way possible including supervising post placement visits. Immediately after speaking with Kay, I called Leah Kushner with Adoption Visions to tell her the good news.

The rest of the week was spent revising our Dear Birth Parent letter and completing a profile, by sorting through pictures and shopping for just the right stationery and stickers. By the time the profile was finished it consisted of eleven pages of family photographs, vacations, birthdays, Christmas and the Dear Birth Parent letter. Each step was agonizing. I wanted the profile to be perfect. It needed to be appealing and genuine. This would be how the prospective birth parents would choose us as a family for their child. Once the profile was completed I had 10 colored copies made. The profiles and application were mailed on March 10, 1998. All that was left to do was to sit back and wait. That was easier said then done when a situation was totally out of your control.

I decided the best thing I could do to occupy my time was surf the adoption web sites. Waiting to be matched was not going to be easy. On one particular day I noticed a post on adoption.com by a Kelly M. "That was odd," I thought. Someone was using my first name and last initial to post or had the same name. When I read the post it revealed an adoptive mother from Wisconsin that had just signed up with Adoption Visions. She was quickly matched through Adoption Visions with a birth mother named Laurel, in Philadelphia, Pennsylvania and her baby was due at the end of September. Another facilitator called Tender Hearts Family Services would be doing the case management. The other Kelly's excitement and emotion was very apparent. I resisted the temptation of emailing her to say congratulations. It was time to head off to work. I knew with so much in common I would have to email her later. Little did I know our two separate worlds were about to become one.

2

Deena

It was Wednesday, April 23, 1998, at approximately 2:30 p.m. I had a board meeting in half an hour and still had some information to collect. Sporadically, the Board of Directors arrived as I was reviewing the agenda for the meeting when the phone rang. Frustrated and reluctant to answer I finally picked up the receiver.

"Hi Kelly, it's Leah, from Adoption Visions. I have some good news. You've been chosen!" she said with excitement.

I began to panic and my mind was racing frantically. Even though Leah was still talking I couldn't believe what I was hearing. Quickly, I grabbed a pen to jot down a few notes. This match was with a prospective birth mother named Deena. She was 34 years old, who had pre-eclampsyia (although she had delivered her other children to term) and might require bed rest during some point of the pregnancy because of her high blood pressure. The birth father's name was Royce. He was a traveling salesman from Ohio and was much older then Deena. How much older was uncertain. Deena lived in Philadelphia, PA and a facilitator by the name of Sonya Furlow DBA Tender Hearts Family Services was doing the case management. Deena was expecting a baby girl on September 1, 1998.

Leah said, "This looks like a really good match Kelly. I will fax you the information and a facilitation agreement. You need to let us know within 24 hours if possible."

"Oh shit," I thought, it was time for the board meeting, and I couldn't concentrate! I told Leah I would let her know our decision after I spoke with Ken. There was no time to call Ken or sit and wait for the fax. The owner of the bank was coming in from Omaha for the meeting so I knew I had to be on time. My mind began to wander. All the thoughts and emotions were so scrambled. I kept thinking, "how in the hell would I be able to concentrate in the meeting when I might be a mom again! Throughout the meeting I was trying to figure out the best way to get a hold of Ken and tell him the news! This was undoubtedly the longest meeting I had ever had, plus the board members were supposed to go out to dinner afterwards.

After the board meeting I hurried back to my office to find the fax from Leah sitting on my desk. Immediately, I contacted the family attorney and faxed the agreement to him. Since the board members were on their way to the country club for dinner I glanced at the clock and realized I was running out of time. After several attempts to call Ken, I gave up and raced down a couple of flights of stairs so I wouldn't be late for dinner.

Walking out the back door of the bank I suddenly realized what a beautiful spring day it really was. Driving south to the country club I spotted Ken's truck heading north toward me. I flagged him down and we pulled off on a side street next to a repair shop. Not as romantic as I had planned "the big moment". But nonetheless, the excitement and thrill were evident. With tears of joy trickling down my face, I jumped out of the car and ran over to Ken's truck where I gave him a big kiss. I then proceeded to share the good news with my husband of four-teen years. I promised to breeze through dinner as quickly as possible. With another quick kiss I passed the fax on to him and scurried back to my car. The poor guy was left in a daze as I raced off to the country club.

Adoption Visions

1628 Josephine St. * Berkeley * CA * 94703

Voice: 510-540-0647   FAX: 510-540-0729   E-mail: Heartweave@aol.com

Kenneth and Kelly,

Congratulations!!

Enclosed is the following:

copy of agreement with Adoption Visions and THFSAC
copy of assessment and update on Deena

Please sign the agreement and fax a copy back to Adoption Visions. Express mail a the
original signed agreement to THFSAC along with two cashier's checks.

Sonya Furlow dba THFSAC $3500
Adoption Visions $2000

Sonya Furlow-THFSAC
7701-Lindberg Blvd. Suite 2102
Philadelphia, PA 19153

I usually set up an introductory phone meeting with the new family and Sonya. Please let
me know what times are good for you so I can arrange this.

Also, Sonya and I have phone meetings each Friday where we discuss each of the birth
mothers. I then provide you with weekly updates on the progress of your birth mother.
During the week if you have any questions regarding your birth mother please e-mail them
to me so I can address them at Fridays meetings.

If you have any questions please feel free to contact me.

Warm Regards

Leah Kushner

You have retained Tender Hearts family Services Adoption Consulting (THFSAC) and Adoption Visions (AV) to facilitate your pursuit of a domestic infant adoption. This document will set forth our agreement with respect to fees and adoption facilitation services and other possible related direct costs, as well as mutual commitments to each other.

This agreement is made between THFSAC and AV and
(Prospective Adoptive Parents, clients).

Adoption Facilitation Agreement

The purpose of Tender Hearts Family Services Adoption Consulting and Adoption Visions is to bring together person desiring to adopt children with birth mothers who have elected to place children for adoption. THFSAC and AV are not an adoption agency and does not purport to act as an adoption agency. Be advised that we do not make decisions for you nor for the birth parents with whom we connect. We do not "select" the client for the birth mother, not the birth mother for the client. It is up to the birth parents of the child to select you as the adoptive parent(s) and for you to agree to accept working with them.

For the purpose of this joint agreement, THFSAC will provide the case management of the birth mother while AV will provide the facilitation between the Client, THFSAC and birth mother. Please direct primary questions to AV. This will allow THFSAC to concentrate on management of birth mothers.

Although service may vary from case to case, the fee includes the following services to Prospective Adoptive Parents:

* Initial interview with Client(s) and orientation on the adoption process
* Discussion of adoptive parent's goals and desires for adoption
* Assistance in preparing your "Birth mother letter" and family profile
* Assistance in locating a child to adopt and screening potential Birth Mothers.
* Presentation and introduction of adoptive parent's portfolio to birth mother
* Comprehensive interaction with Birth Mother to determine her commitment level, explain the adoption process and counsel her
* Obtain background information on the Birth parents (including health, ethnic background and social history)
* Obtain proof of pregnancy from a prospective Birth Mother
* Assisting Clients in obtaining medical coverage for the Birth Mother
* Arranging medical care for the Birth Mother
* Attendance at the hospital by THFSAC social worker and/or adoption advisor following the birth of the child unless distance precludes attendance
* Assisting Prospective Adoptive Parents with engaging the proper legal and/or agency professionals to complete the adoption process
* Interface with attorney and/or agency finalizing adoption

The birth mother and the prospective adoptive family must come to an agreement with respect to the nature and extent of future contact among the member of the triad (birth mother, adoptive parents and the child) if the Birth Mother requests this.

THFSAC and AV may obtain information about situations from the Birth mother or referring social services agency, and/or professionals. THFSAC may also obtain information concerning but not limited to, the birthmother's medical and social history, use of drugs, cigarettes and alcohol before and during pregnancy, financial status or needs, insurance coverage and identify and medical social history and whereabouts of alleged, legal and/or presumed birth father. THFSAC and AV do not perform investigation service, but will under the direction of the client have such services performed by a professional and the clients will assume such cost involved. THFSAC and AV cannot and does not guarantee that any circumstances surrounding an adoption plan will remain the same during anytime in the period of the adoption plan.

It shall be the responsibility of the Adoptive Parents to retain an attorney and/or licensed adoption agency to process the independent adoption in a court of jurisdiction. Adoptive Parents shall be responsible for all fees related to the finalization of the adoption. Adoptive Parents are hereby informed that it may be necessary for the Adoptive Parents to hire separate legal counsel for the birth mother, according to the laws of the state she resides in. Please be advised that, for separate and additional fees, you will need to seek the legal advice and services of a licensed adoption agency and/or a competent adoption attorney in your state and/or the state where the birth parents reside in, in order to assure that you will be able to legally adopt the child you locate.

THFSAC and AV strongly suggests that the Clients do not commit to, or provide any financial assistance to, any birth mother., hire an agency or attorney to represent her, or buy transportation for the purpose of meeting her, without advice from their adoption attorney or adoption agency. Clients are encouraged to consult with their adoption attorney for direction and possible exceptions in accordance with the laws of the states involved. Clients are advised to consider purchasing ADOPTION TERMINATION INSURANCE to protect themselves whenever supporting a birth mother financially.

It is not the responsibility of THFSAC and AV to advise you in the laws or procedures of adoption in your state, nor any other state, nor to engage in the unlicensed practice of law in the field of adoption. You are advised to rely solely on the competent and professional legal advice, once you have connected with birth parents and you wish to proceed with adoption.

Clients understand that THFSAC and AV cannot and doesn't give any guarantee as to the final outcome of any given adoption plan. THFSAC and AV cannot and does not guarantee the physical, emotional, mental condition of any child or children involved in any adoption.

Client's efforts to adopt can sometimes result in failure. It is specifically agreed that any such failure will not be grounds for a refund of any part of any fees paid. This Agreement acknowledges that each party understands that there are significant risks: that there may be financial loss, that either of the birth parents may change their mind, either before or after the birth of the baby, before or after consent or relinquishment papers are signed.

The birth mother and the prospective adoptive family must come to an agreement with respect to the nature and extent of future contact among the member of the triad (birth mother, adoptive parents and the child) if the Birth Mother requests this.

THFSAC and AV may obtain information about situations from the Birth mother or referring social services agency, and/or professionals. THFSAC may also obtain information concerning but not limited to, the birthmother's medical and social history, use of drugs, cigarettes and alcohol before and during pregnancy, financial status or needs, insurance coverage and identify and medical social history and whereabouts of alleged, legal and/or presumed birth father. THFSAC and AV do not perform investigation service, but will under the direction of the client have such services performed by a professional and the clients will assume such cost involved. THFSAC and AV cannot and does not guarantee that any circumstances surrounding an adoption plan will remain the same during anytime in the period of the adoption plan.

It shall be the responsibility of the Adoptive Parents to retain an attorney and/or licensed adoption agency to process the independent adoption in a court of jurisdiction. Adoptive Parents shall be responsible for all fees related to the finalization of the adoption. Adoptive Parents are hereby informed that it may be necessary for the Adoptive Parents to hire separate legal counsel for the birth mother, according to the laws of the state she resides in. Please be advised that, for separate and additional fees, you will need to seek the legal advice and services of a licensed adoption agency and/or a competent adoption attorney in your state and/or the state where the birth parents reside in, in order to assure that you will be able to legally adopt the child you locate.

THFSAC and AV strongly suggests that the Clients do not commit to, or provide any financial assistance to, any birth mother., hire an agency or attorney to represent her, or buy transportation for the purpose of meeting her, without advice from their adoption attorney or adoption agency. Clients are encouraged to consult with their adoption attorney for direction and possible exceptions in accordance with the laws of the states involved. Clients are advised to consider purchasing ADOPTION TERMINATION INSURANCE to protect themselves whenever supporting a birth mother financially.

It is not the responsibility of THFSAC and AV to advise you in the laws or procedures of adoption in your state, nor any other state, nor to engage in the unlicensed practice of law in the field of adoption. You are advised to rely solely on the competent and professional legal advice, once you have connected with birth parents and you wish to proceed with adoption.

Clients understand that THFSAC and AV cannot and doesn't give any guarantee as to the final outcome of any given adoption plan. THFSAC and AV cannot and does not guarantee the physical, emotional, mental condition of any child or children involved in any adoption.

Client's efforts to adopt can sometimes result in failure. It is specifically agreed that any such failure will not be grounds for a refund of any part of any fees paid. This Agreement acknowledges that each party understands that there are significant risks: that there may be financial loss, that either of the birth parents may change their mind, either before or after the birth of the baby, before or after consent or relinquishment papers are signed.

However, all parties hereby agree to use their best efforts to effectuate and expedite the purpose of this Agreement. In the event of a "failed" or "disrupted" adoption Clients will not be charged a second fee for further services, as covered by this Agreement.

Parties agree that if a dispute arises out of the performance of services render under this Agreement, the matter will be submitted to binding arbitration. The parties agree to the mutual selection of an arbitrator. If agreement cannot be reached, the dispute will be submitted to the American Arbitration Association and will be arbitrated in accordance with the rules of the American Arbitration Association. The parties to this Agreement agree to settle all disputes through binding arbitration, waiving all right to pursue court action.

THFSAC and AV will act on the behalf to he adoptive parents, also referred to as Clients, who are party to this Agreement. This Agreement may not be transferred or sold.

THFSAC and AV will be paid a program fee of $10,000 which includes the following itemized and fee schedule.

Itemized Fees

THFSAC Case Management	$ 6000
Adoption Visions Program Fee	$ 2000
Office Expenses	$ 500
Birth mother living expenses	$ 1500*
Total	$10,000

Fees are due as follows:

Upon commitment of adoption referral	$5500
8th Month of Pregnancy	$2500
Upon Custody of the Baby	$2000

* If the birth mothers living expenses exceeds $2000 the clients will be required to pay the living expenses in excess of $2000 and will be notified in advance of the fees.
If the birth mothers living expenses are below $1500 the clients will be refunded the unused portion upon finalization of their adoption.

Adoptions cost and fees NOT included in the THFSAC and AV fee, may be, but are not limited to: any and all Birth mother-related expenses (medical, legal, psychiatric and maintenance expenses as they may be reasonable and necessary) over $2000, attorney fees, adoption agency fees, counseling fees, adoption service provider fees or any other professional party.

Deena, EDC: 09.01.98

Tender Hearts Family Services

Deena
EDC—9.1.98
EDC—sono

_____

_____

Initial Assessment and Motivation: I initially met Deena on 2.23.98 and again on 3.3.98. Deena is 14 weeks pregnant (3 months). Deena is the mother of three children and has a history of pre-eclampsyia and edema, but has had three healthy babies. She had pre-natal visit on 3.2.98 and her blood pressure was normal. She will be leaving work for short-term disability around the end of March. **Deena states that she has decided on an adoption plan for her unborn child because she cannot emotionally or financially care for a fourth child.**

Expectant Mother's Description: Deena was born January 5, 1964 in Philadelphia, Pennsylvania. She is five feet, four inches tall and her normal weight is 120 pounds. She has blonde hair and brown eyes. She is of English and French background and has no knowledge of Native American heritage of any kind. She has never been married.

Family/Personal Hx: Deena's parents are retired and live with her older sister in Arizona. She speaks to them monthly on the telephone, but has not seen them for several years. Deena's oldest two children have the same father. The youngest child has a different father. She has been struggling to raise them on her own and has been on and off welfare.

History of Present Pregnancy: Deena has been sexually involved with Royce, a casual friend, who lives in Ohio, for a few years. He is aware of the pregnancy and supports an adoption plan.

Past Medical Hx: Deena states that she is in good health and has only been hospitalized for the births of her children. She currently has private medical insurance.

HIV Risk Factor and Substance Use: Deena has been tested for HIV during routine pre-natal examination. She denies any drug or alcohol use.

Walking into the country club grinning from ear to ear, the excitement was written all over my face. I have been known to wear my emotions on my shirtsleeves and this was no exception. This was a big board meeting. Even though I could hardly contain myself, as the only woman on the board of directors I knew that in this man's world I needed to regain my composure and professionalism. Repeatedly, I kept telling myself to stay calm, cool and collected.

A co-worker of eight years immediately noticed my facial expression and quickly asked. "What's up?" That was all it took. I had always felt I could trust him and of course spilled out the good news. What a relief it was to finally share my exciting news and moments later I was congratulated by the entire group of board members. Unfortunately, I left out the part asking him to keep the good news quiet for that moment.

Upon arriving home Ken and I discussed the facilitators agreement and the next steps we should take. After such an exhausting and exciting day, sleep was hard to come by. Yet the next morning I awoke refreshed and enthused. I called Leah to inquire about Sonya Furlow. Who was she? What was her part in this adoption? Leah told me she worked with Sonya before and described her as a compassionate woman who really took a personal interest in her birth mothers. Sonya was a single mother of one adopted son and she had experienced a couple of failed adoptions herself, which may have added to her sensitivity. Often she invited prospective birth mothers to her home for meals and when she was able she personally took them to their doctors' appointments.

Our attorney stopped by my office with Leah's agreement. His big warning was if Deena changed her mind we could be out some money. It was evident he was leery about the situation and had not encountered a situation like it before. As instructed, I faxed the agreement to Leah and purchased two cashier's checks. One check to Adoption Visions for $2000.00 then the other in the amount of $3500.00 to Sonya Furlow DBA Tender Hearts Family Services. Leah, of Adoption Visions, stated she would set up an initial conference call with Sonya for the next day and then Adoption Visions would send us weekly updates on Deena.

Leah told me that although Sonya was very busy with her prospective birth mothers, they had weekly conference calls on the progress of their mutual clients.

The next morning we were scheduled to call Sonya. The phone rang several times before she finally answered. I was somewhat surprised that her voice was flat and monotone, our conversation lasted less than two minutes. Sonya reported she'd hurt her back the night before and that she was in a great deal of pain. She said she would pass her updates of Deena to Leah and not wanting to be too pushy we didn't try to extend the conversation.

We were not impressed with Sonya and we felt uncomfortable with the conversation. Even though the phone call didn't meet our expectations at least we were relieved to know that Sonya was a real person.

◆   ◆   ◆

We were aware Deena could change her mind at any time about proceeding through with the adoption plan, but for our own peace of mind we needed to think positive. With that thought looming in the back of my mind I began to concentrate and prepare for Deena's upcoming birth. I began thinking of the nursery and making plans to take 12 weeks off from work when the baby was born. As the days progressed I started living for the weekly computer updates from Leah at Adoption Visions. Gradually we began to tell a few close friends, family and co-workers of the upcoming event. The excitement was infectious and Kassie became excited too. She changed her prayers to include Deena and the baby.

Then it dawned on me. Our baby was due September 1st. The other Kelly that was posting on the Internet, her baby was due the end of September and in Philly too! I had to email the Kelly in Wisconsin. Once we made a connection there was an instant chemistry from the first emails. We began to forge a friendship and rapidly learned we had much more in common besides Adoption Visions and Sonya Furlow. We both anticipated hearing from one another and supported each other during the "waiting period". Ironically, Adoption Visions tended to have difficulty keeping the two of us straight. I had not received our weekly update from Leah and after a week of waiting I called her to see how Deena was. Leah quickly began talking about Laurel. I interrupted her in mid sentence to let her know she had had gotten me mixed up with Kelly Motl and I was matched with Deena.

By May of 1998, the weekly updates on Deena had stopped. I was anxious, couldn't stand the waiting and unknown so I decided I would call Leah. After several attempts in contacting her we finally connected. Leah reported that, Sonya was too busy with her prospective birth mothers and she would only be sending us monthly updates. She also informed me that if we had any questions not to email Sonya, contact her instead. All she knew was Deena had been placed on total bed rest.

The waiting and wondering became unbearable. Unanswered questions continually ran through my mind. What did Deena look like? What would the baby look like? Would the baby be healthy? A picture of Deena was supposed to have been sent weeks ago. Leah had suggested that we send Deena cards or small gifts like magazines or puzzles to help lift her spirits. Ken and I knew this had to be an emotional and frustrating time for Deena. So we began to send weekly cards. Some were just thinking of you, hope you feel better soon and just a note to say hi. A great amount of effort was put into choosing just the right cards and finding small gifts. I searched all the stores in town gathering bookmarks, postcards, puzzles and magazines. Being hundreds of miles away from Deena the very least I could do was let her know we cared and were continually thinking about her. Deena wanted a closed adoption and we wanted to respect her decision yet be there to support her through the pregnancy. Frustration and helplessness soon set in. Each day consisted of emailing the other Kelly and waiting for the monthly updates. Feeling isolated I decided a shopping spree in Lincoln, NE was just what I needed to escape.

I knew not to buy too much for the baby, since Deena could still decide to parent her child. The trip to Kohl's was just too much for me to resist, as I found the most wonderful little dress. The bodice was soft, fine, white terry cloth with a light pink satin bow on the front. The skirt of the dress was a light pink cotton material with patterns of small dark rose buds. The baby had to have a coming home outfit! Being a stickler for having things match I quickly found a matching rosebud bonnet, socks, and a soft white blanket showered with small rosebuds. Once again I felt optimistic and excited. When I arrived home the first thing on my agenda was to email Kelly Motl about the adorable little outfit I had just purchased. Feeling positive I felt it was time to talk to Ken about a name for the baby.

As the first of July rolled around the excitement soon turned into turmoil and sleepless nights, when Sonya suddenly called me.

"Hi Kelly, this is Sonya" Panic struck! Sonya I thought, Oh my, she has never called us before! Sonya went on to say, "with Deena on total bed rest she has had a lot of time to think. She is having mixed feelings about the adoption plan. This is natural for most birth mothers. She has three older children that are out of control and very mean to her. They want Deena to keep the baby. I wanted you to know that you and Ken can call me anytime."

"Sonya, what about Royce? We do not know much about him. Is he helping Deena with her kids?" I asked.

"Kelly, Royce has not had contact with Deena for several months, actually since she made the decision to proceed with an adoption plan back in February. I have met Royce and he is 50 something and looks like that one pro golf player." Sonya replied.

"Which one?" I questioned.

"I can't think of his name but you know he always wears that one hat. Deena met Royce when she was working as a receptionist. She has always claimed he has been very nice to her. He took her once to Las Vegas on a business trip, but other then that I don't know anything else personal about him. Deena does think he may be married." She stated.

"Sonya, we were suppose to have received a picture of Deena and we still haven't received it yet." I said.

"Oh gosh Kelly. I didn't send it?" She questioned with a panicked tone.

"No." I stated matter of fact.

"My short-term memory is terrible. I will get it sent out right away. I am sorry. I have just been so busy. I have one homeless birth mother living with me now. I am trying to find her a place and get her back on her feet. Her parents are not supportive whatsoever. I need to run Kelly, I have another assessment in a few minutes." She replied.

"Thanks for calling Sonya." I said.

"Kelly you and Ken take care and don't worry, God has a plan and a baby for you." Sonya said with compassion.

Immediately at the beginning of the phone conversation my stomach began to churn. What the hell? We were in limbo once again. We had no control over our future and were left with no other option then to trust that the adoption professionals were doing the best they could. Will she or won't she? Forgetting about supper I grabbed a beer from the refrigerator and ran downstairs to email the other Kelly. Tears began to well in my eyes as I was typing. "Think positive" I thought. From that point every waking moment, every sleepless night, I began to slip further into the dark tunnel of obsession. Day by day I became oblivious to everything but the adoption plan. Finally, the picture of Deena arrived. No letter, just the picture. That was enough. No that was great! Finally I had something tangible.

Deena was small framed, with straight shoulder length light brown, blondish hair. She was wearing a western outfit standing next to a couple of cowboys. I wondered if one of the men was Royce. Deena was cute and looked like a happy person. She had a nice smile and blue or green eyes. I tucked the picture into my leather briefcase. Continually, I would take the picture out and stare at it as loads of questions reeled through my mind. Yet it gave me a connection to the woman who was in my thoughts and prayers.

Suddenly another spark of hope! In the middle of July I checked my email. There was a message from a young woman considering adoption, who had seen our profile on adoption.com. She had completed an adoption plan before, was the mother of three children and pregnant and searching for adoptive parents. My heart skipped several beats. I wanted to know more about the young woman named Angel and her family. She had sent us an email with her picture. She was petite and had long brown hair with big blue eyes. The best part of all she was from Nebraska. As weeks passed we formed an online friendship. Angel was very open and easy to talk too. I was totally open and honest with her about Deena. Angel's baby was due mid September and after several weeks of emailing her we met at a shopping mall in Omaha. She was so different then Deena. Angel wanted a totally open adoption and had an open adoption with the adoptive parents of her first daughter. I just couldn't believe how well we connected and what a simply lovely young woman she was. Angel was fairly certain she wanted an adoption plan for her child. At that point it really didn't matter, we didn't press Angel and wanted her to take her time and do what was best for her and her unborn baby. I knew no matter what her decision would be I had met a truly wonderful friend.

As August approached, fear and anxiety set in. I was afraid to leave the house, as I might miss a phone call or an email. Weekend camping trips had always been a big part of our lives. Even time off camping didn't help relieve the stress and multitude of emotions. I could not let my mind or my heart stray from the thoughts of the upcoming births. Camping only freed up more time to dwell on the what if, why's and how's. Ken began to handle the adoption differently. He seemed to be more relaxed yet concerned that I was becoming so obsessed. Trying to get me to leave the house for the weekends was getting harder as time went on.

Too add fuel to the fire on August 6th we received an email from Sonya.

"Ken, its instructions on picking up the baby! We need a name for her! We need an attorney! Sonya recommends Jay Ginsburg in Philly. See look at the email." I rambled with all the excitement I could muster.

With no emotion apparent on his face Ken read the email.

Subject: Instructions for Picking Up Baby
Date: Thu, 6 Aug 1998 22:11:59 EDT
From: THFSAC@aol.com
To: Kelly Mostrom
CC: Heartweave@aol.com

Tender Hearts Family Services, Inc.
7707 Lindbergh Blvd. Suite 2101
Philadelphia, PA 19153
215-552-8539
Fax: 215-937-4328
Email: THFSAC@aol.com

Instructions for Picking Up Your Baby Born in the Philadelphia, Pennsylvania Area

Your Birth mother, Deena is expected to deliver her baby around September 1, 1998 at Thomas Jefferson University Hospital 11th & Chestnut, Philadelphia. She has stated that she is committed to the adoption plan, but you may want to wait until she signed the relinquishment papers before traveling to Pennsylvania.

You may want to think about an attorney here in Pennsylvania and/or an agency. I recommend Jay Ginsburg. You may select anyone to take the legal terminations from the birth parents, please advise me whom you have engaged. You should be able to pay for this service once arriving in Pennsylvania, just in case one or both of the birth parents decide not to sign. If you would like for me to arrange this service for you, please let me know. Mr. Ginsburg is very familiar with the court system here in Eastern Pennsylvania and works with Choices Adoption Agency, which will file the Interstate Compact Papers. I estimate these fees to be about $1500.

There are several hotel chains in Philadelphia. I suggest the Extended Stay America; in Philadelphia they are located near Philadelphia International Airport. Reservations and information call 1 800 EXT STAY. Direct number to Philadelphia Hotel is 215.492.6766. Your estimated stay in Philadelphia is 3-10 days. Please let me know where you are staying as soon as you can.

Please review the attached Adoptive Parent Checklist. Any questions, please contact me.

Sonya Furlow, Tender Hearts Family Services, Inc.

After reading the email, Ken was more skeptical; I knew he was guarding himself from hurt and disappointment. Nevertheless, I called Jay Ginsburg. What a wonderful man was my first impression. After a lengthy conversation I found Mr. Ginsburg to be a knowledgeable and compassionate attorney. I discussed our conversation with Ken and explained that Mr. Ginsburg had some other clients that were also working with Sonya. He was a member of the American Academy of Adoption Attorney's. His office assistant was also expecting a baby soon, so she would be calling to get some additional information from us. With a big smile on my face I said, "Oh and Ken, I will need to give his assistant a name for the baby."

I called Sonya to let her know that we were very impressed with Mr. Ginsburg and he would be the attorney representing us when the time came.

"Sonya how is Deena?" I asked.

"Uh, well you know, she is still unsure. The baby might have to go to cradle care for a while. She's still on bed rest and has a nurse stopping by a couple of times a week to check her blood pressure." She replied without emotion.

"Sonya I am going crazy here wondering what is going on. Has she mentioned us at all?" I questioned.

"No, not really other then to tell you thanks for the cards and things. Kelly you can call me every week for an update. Do you have a name picked out?" She asked.

"Yes, Ken and I just decided on Kloe Martis, Martis is Ken's father's middle name. How are you and your son?" I asked.

"We are fine. Marcus is being an ornery little cuss tonight. I've been so busy he's been staying at my mom's a lot. We really need to go to church this Sunday, the priest and nuns have been wondering where I have been. Marcus! Don't do that! Kelly, I better go. You take care and call me next week." She replied.

"Alright, thanks Sonya." I stated.

Each day seemed longer then the day before. I tried calling Sonya several times the following week. There was no answer. Finally, my patience was gone; I began calling the first thing in the morning and continued throughout the day until I could get more then just the answering machine. Coupled with phone calls I also sent several emails in hopes that Sonya would take just a few minutes of her busy schedule and send at least a tidbit of information on Deena. Finally! Sonya emailed us saying Deena's blood pressure went up and she had been admitted to the hospital. Deena started labor and was requesting the baby go into cradle care until she made a decision. I began calling repeatedly for the next couple of days. I was impatient and relentless; yet at the same time afraid I would offend Sonya by calling so much or say something wrong and upset her. Still there was no giving up until I finally got an answer.

Sonya answered the phone out of breath. She was just getting home from the hospital. Deena's contractions had stopped, although the baby had flipped and her foot was in the birth canal. The doctors were trying to get the baby to turn.

Sonya said, "Kelly do you know of anyone that would want a 6 month old ½ Hispanic and ½ Caucasian baby boy?" She asked.

"Yes! Me!" I exclaimed.

"I will go ahead and present your profile and we will see what happens with Deena. I will contact Mr. Ginsburg so he can start some of the paperwork just in case Deena decides to proceed with the adoption plan. I need to run but I will be in touch." Sonya stated.

"Sonya call me as soon as you know anything!" I said.

"I will, get some sleep Kelly." She replied.

Sleep, yeah, right I thought. The next two weeks took forever. On August 25th we received an email from Sonya.

"Kelly, had a chance to speak to Jay Ginsburg about the situation. He cannot file the paperwork with the court until day 40 after terminations have been signed. Deena does not want to sign immediately, she wants the baby to go to foster care if possible then when she has had time to deal with the other kids, she will sign and the baby can either go home with you or remain in foster care until he files with the court and the judge signs off, which can be about another 30 days so the baby will be about 2 ½ months. The baby should be born sometime with the next 24 hours; I will talk to you later. I have pulled out your profile to send to a couple of birth mothers out-of-state and to show to birth moms I have here. I want to work on re-matching now, so you can have a placement quickly."
Sonya

Even though her email wasn't an encouraging one I still maintained hope that once the baby was born Deena would continue with the adoption plan. The situation was totally out of our control and hope was all I had left to hold on too.

Even though miles separated us, in my own mind I had formed a relationship and commitment to Deena and her child.

A few hours later Sonya called to briefly let us know Kloe Martis had arrived into the world weighing 6 pounds 12 ounces. Such an innocent child, I thought. Sonya was on her way to the hospital to see Deena and Kloe. I paced the floors frantically waiting for Sonya to call us back. Deep down inside I had been diligently praying that after giving birth Deena would suddenly know what her decision would be. As the day went on my anxiety level grew with every passing hour that Sonya did not call us back.

The next day I made several attempts to reach Sonya by phone when finally she answered. Sonya had just walked into her apartment from the hospital. With disgust in her voice Sonya told me that Royce showed up with Deena's three older children.

"The kids are brats! That oldest one, he must be about 13 or 14 got right into Deena's face and called her a selfish bitch! The children took turns holding the baby and treated her like a rag doll. The kids are extremely upset because Deena has an adoption plan. She will be discharged in a day or two and the baby will go to cradle care." She maintained.

We were devastated to say the least. Yet for some reason I still had hope. After all, that was all I had left to hold onto. Kloe was still in cradle care and things could change. Soon, September had arrived; daily I waited for an email or phone call to see if there was any news on Kloe. Two weeks from the date of Deena being discharge, from the hospital, Royce finally gave up and returned to Ohio to work. He called Sonya frequently checking on Deena and Kloe. He didn't think it was right to leave the baby in cradle care. At the end of September Sonya called to let me know Royce had confided in her. The reason he did not speak about his past was that he had a son that died a tragic death and he was not comfortable talking about it. He was not married. At that moment, Royce was on his way to meet with Sonya so they could drive to the cradle care home to pick up Kloe. Royce wanted to force the issue with Deena. He didn't feel it was right for Kloe to be staying in cradle care those all-important first days of her life. "It is time for Deena to decide," he said.

Later that night Sonya called. When they arrived at Deena's home the kids began to pass the baby around like a rag doll and Deena just ignored her. When Royce confronted Deena and told her the baby had to come home and it was time to make a choice. Her response was "whatever." Sonya said she then left and called the Department of Human Services. DHS would open a file on Deena and the baby, and would watch them closely for the next six months.

I was by now totally depressed and mourning the child that was not meant to be a part of our family. Still there was a small shred of hope that just maybe, Deena would continue with the adoption plan. It was so hard for the whole family and our friends. Everyone had been praying and anticipating the new arrival. We continued to hang on to the hope that God had a plan for us. Kassie was so disappointed. Tears streamed down her face when I told her. She was such a wise and innocent child she continued to pray for Deena and her baby and that God would find her a new brother or sister. All along we had been honest with Kassie that she may or may not be a big sister. We wanted to tread lightly and protect her from the possible devastation, yet at the same time we wanted to prepare her that our home and our lives could change and it would be different when she was no longer an only child.

Even through the sadness and despair we still had a glimmer of hope. Maybe Deena would change her mind. That thought always would race back through my mind. And perhaps if we weren't meant to parent Deena's child we knew God had plan. Angel was due at any time and maybe that was the path He was leading us towards. Did he mean for us to parent a child in an open adoption with a wonderful person and new friend?

We had not heard from Angel for a couple of weeks. Then at the end of September we received an email that Angel had given birth to a baby boy on September 17th. She and her boyfriend had decided to parent. It was obvious it was very difficult for her to tell us. Though we were sad and shed some tears we were comfortable with Angel's decision. Partially because we knew her on a more intimate level and knew that she only wanted the best for her child. She was a good mom and loved all her children very much. Angel and I continued to email each other and maintained our friendship.

Feeling alone and lost I continued to email Kelly in Wisconsin. No one seemed to understand the emotional roller coaster ride we had been on, other then Kelly. She also became leery and afraid that same thing that happened to Ken and I would also happen to her and Steve. I was desperately hoping and praying that their baby would arrive home soon. We both begin to wonder about Sonya and her legitimacy. I made several phones calls to the Better Business Bureau in Philadelphia to see if any complaints had been filed against Sonya. The BBB had an automated phone system. All I had to do was simply dial the phone number of her business and the automated system would respond. Being suspicious I had also checked her home phone number. Sonya and her business came back clean, "No reports". That was a good sign I thought. The twinge of suspicion had subsided.

As October 1998 rolled around Kelly and Steve Motl's adoption had also failed. During our grieving period our friendship became stronger and we relied heavily on each other to navigate through our emotions. Friends and family seemed to have empathy but unless they had been in a similar situation it was very difficult for them to truly understand our personal trials and tribulations. We frequently checked with each other on the stories and information being told to us by Sonya. We felt as though if she was pulling a scam on us we would be able to catch her if she was lying to us. When speaking with Sonya we both pretended not to know the intimate details of each other's situations. We considered this our own private safety net, just in case something would go awry.

3

Roxanne

At the end of October 1998, Sonya had emailed us with three prospective birth mothers that all had chosen us and we were told to choose one. Feeling uneasy about the situation we were presented I called Sonya. She reassured us that all three women loved us and were requesting to be presented to her three families that had failed adoptions. With much thought and excitement we chose Roxanne. According to Sonya's email she was twenty-two years old, weighed 140 pounds prior to her pregnancy and was five feet three inches tall. She had brown hair, and brown eyes. Her due date was February 18, 1999 and she was the single mother of three children, two boys and a girl.

Upon confirmation with Roxanne Sonya fax her assessment to us. It stated that Roxanne was receiving welfare, and would be required to be in the state job training programs by March of 1999. She was pregnant by her second child's father, Tyler, who was twenty-four years old and facing county jail time of eleven and a half to twenty three months for driving under the influence and other pending charges. According to Sonya, county time was not considered a big crime in Philadelphia. Tyler was aware of the adoption plan, and he questioned paternity, but agreed to sign the relinquishments. The report also included preliminary findings from her prenatal visits showing that Roxanne had prenatal care since her second month, had tested negative for alcohol, cigarettes, and other drugs. Her current medical information was completed but not typed and that information would be forthcoming.

We were excited, to say the least. Maybe the other failed adoptions were because God was telling us to be patient, and that our child would come when the time was right. Sonya had told us she would also continue showing our profile to other prospective birth mothers since we had already had a failed adoption. She emphasized continuously that she wanted our baby to come home as quickly as possible.

I had decided with the second match with a prospective birth mother I would be more proactive with my communication with Sonya. Ken and I both felt we should be having contact with Sonya on a weekly basis. That was what we did. I would email Sonya on a consistent basis requesting medical history and an update on Roxanne's condition. Many times she wouldn't respond by email, so I would begin calling. Being totally focused on the adoption I would constantly call her at home or her office phone number, however I didn't always leave a message on her voice mail when she didn't answer. Instead I would redial her number throughout the day until she would personally answer the phone.

Rapidly Sonya and I developed a friendship. She often shared stories about her son Marcus who was also adopted and was about four years old. Her mother lived close by and often babysat for her and on some occasions did respite care or cradle care for some of her birth mothers and adoptive parents. Sonya's parents were divorced but she was close to both of them.

By November 3rd, Sonya was extremely busy and had contacted us to let us know she was trying to obtain medical information and consents from Tyler. Roxanne had apparently given her some misinformation on Tyler. Sonya was setting up a meeting with him to get the details ironed out. In the meantime she informed us she had presented our profile to another prospective birth mother named Andrea. She was sixteen years old, a cheerleader, and lived on the east coast. Andrea and her mother were trying to decide between Ken and I and a couple that lived near them. Several weeks later we were told that Andrea had chosen the east coast family. Sonya told us "Don't worry, I have another birth mom named Bonnie due in late December, I will show her your profile along with two other families that have had failed adoptions." I knew immediately Kelly and Steve had to be one of the other couples. They had just been matched with another prospective birth mom named Gloria.

A pang of competition flared up. Of course I wanted Kelly and Steve to find their son or daughter, but I didn't like feeling that we were competing against each other. I decided it was best not to discuss too much about Bonnie with Kelly. Certainly after all we had been through I didn't want competition to be an issue between us.

Just before Christmas we received the assessments on Tyler. When Sonya had a meeting with him, she found him to be nothing like Roxanne described. Tyler had taken awhile to finish the paperwork because he wanted his attorney to review the information first. Sonya described him to us as an "investment banker, tall, physically fit, with model looks." It was determined his brush with the law involved numerous DUI offenses and he spent several weekends in county jail.

Tyler was getting married on February 14th, 1999 to his current girlfriend and was supportive of the adoption plan. It was apparent at her meeting with him that he felt the adoption plan was in the best interest of the baby.

Of course Ken and I were ecstatic. Tyler appeared to be a young man with a bright future and was very supportive of the adoption plan. On December 24th we received an email:

Kelly, Roxanne had her ultrasound…the baby is a boy! Merry Christmas! Sonya

We already had a daughter and we were open to any sex but how lucky could we be? Christmas was filled with anticipation and hope. Then on New Years Eve Sonya sent another email. Her sister-in-law died suddenly and she would be traveling to Florida for a week. She wrote in an email "I haven't been this upset since my husband died. She and I were very close."

Upon her returning home from Florida, she once again sent us an email to let us know Bonnie had chosen another family. Then we received another email from Sonya that was directed toward all of her clients, which read:

Subject: Re: Jay Ginsburg
Date: Mon, 11 Jan 1999 09:47:38 EST
From: THFSAC@aol.com
To: THFSAC@aol.com

Dear Families: Please do not contact my associate Jay Ginsburg, Esq. Without speaking to me first. Jay does not get birth mother files until after she signs the consents. He is receiving an overabundance of calls from my clients for information, and most times legal advice. If I am aware that you are calling, I can fax him information on the birth mother that you are matched with. He only charges $1200 + court cost for Pennsylvania terminations of birth parents. I am the one who actually takes the consents from the birth parents. If you have called Jay more than twice or spoke to him at length, I am asking you to send a check for $250 to offset his time and resources. Please make the check payable to him, BUT send it to me. I need a copy for my files, I will forward to him. He is not asking for any prepayment. I will deduct this amount from your balance when you come for your child. Any questions, please feel free to contact me. Mr. Ginsburg is a wonderful and great attorney. Thanking you in advance for your consideration, Sonya

This email caused some questions and Kelly Motl and I speculated on what it had meant. The next day I had forgotten about it as Sonya faxed us Tyler's medical assessment, which was followed by an email that she was presenting us to another prospective birth mom, named Brandi.

Subject: Re: Thanks for the fax!
Date: Wed, 13 Jan 1999 02:23:42 EST
From: THFSAC@aol.com
To: Kelly Mostrom

Kelly, I have an unusual situation. I have a birth mom due 1.21.99. The family she is matched with has decided to take another baby. Brandi is devastated because she had a good relationship with the family. She is unsure of what she wants to do now. She has four kids already and she is very young, 21 years old. I do not want you to flip, but I want you to be prepared if she wants to continue with the placement of the child. I have the profiles ready. She will see only adoptive parents who have had a failed adoption plan. Hopefully she will love you to death. Could you write her a brief note and email it to me? I can fax her assessment if you would like to see it. The birth father has already signed consents, Sonya

Quickly I sat down to write Brandi a note. Fretting over every word and wanting to say the right thing sent me into another tailspin. The ups and downs of this emotional roller coaster were taking their toll. I was becoming narrow-sighted and it was increasingly difficult for me to think about anything else. My concentration at work was almost non-existent. Each morning the bank staff greeted me and we would chat about the adoption and what was transpiring. It became evident to them that my heart and soul was consumed by the pending adoption and not with work. Four days later we received another email from Sonya.

Subject: Legal Counsel/PA Terminations
Date: Sun, 17 Jan 1999 14:16:59 EST
From: THFSAC@aol.com
To: THFSAC@aol.com

Dear Clients: Due to his schedule as a Judicial Master, Replacement Judge, and his current law practice, Jay Ginsburg, Esq. Is not to be contacted directly by you or your legal counsel in your home state. You and your legal counsel must contact Tender Hearts. If Mr. Ginsburg is contacted by you or your legal representative without my prior knowledge this can or will be terms for terminating the adoption process. If you have any questions please call me.

Sonya Furlow, MSW, Tender Hearts Family Services. 01.17.99

Upon receiving yet another email directed to all of Sonya's clients Kelly and I began to speculate and wonder if something major had happened with one of Sonya's clients. Besides feeling uneasy about the recent emails Kelly and Steve were not comfortable with their prospective birth mother Gloria. Kelly was hoping that Brandi would choose them and felt they were a better fit with Brandi. It was important to them to have an open adoption.

I called Sonya to see what was going on and she chalked up the events to a couple of adoptive mothers continuingly contacting Mr. Ginsburg when he didn't have access to the complete files and was extremely busy with his law practice. After her brief explanation Sonya had informed me that Roxanne had questions about how we would explain the adoption to our child, what our thoughts were on discipline and what we felt about her making an adoption plan. Ken and I spent a great deal of time preparing a letter for Roxanne and mailed it to Sonya as soon as we could.

Anxiously I waited for some kind of acknowledgement from Sonya that she had received the letter that was intended for Roxanne. After several days passed I had still not heard from her. I was filled with anxiety and not sleeping at night. I desperately wanted to know about Roxanne's reaction to our letter and make sure she was still confident with choosing us to parent her child.

Finally by the first of February I reached Sonya by phone.

"I am sorry Kelly, I changed my phone number and the phone company had messed up my phone lines." She told me.

"Sonya, I want to know how Roxanne is doing, and what did she think of our letter?" I asked.

"She was fine with it Kelly. I think we should set up a conference call with you guys and Roxanne, how about on the fourth about 4:00 p.m.?" Sonya inquired.

"Oh Sonya, what do we say to her?" I asked with panic creeping into my voice.

Sonya replied, "Just be yourself, it will be fine. Brandi has still not chosen a family and I am not sure she will, she is still upset about the other couple backing out."

Ken and I quickly adjusted our schedule to make sure we would be available for the conference call. We waited and waited; every minute the phone didn't ring seemed like an hour. Finally, I couldn't take it anymore; it was an hour past the originally scheduled time frame. My stomach was in knots and I was afraid something happened so I called Sonya. She sounded out of breath and told us she had just gotten home from the hospital and would call us back. We waited another two hours for Sonya to return our phone call. After pacing the floors she finally returned our call but unfortunately by the time she had contacted Roxanne it was too late. Roxanne was sleeping and one of her children answered the phone. Sonya said we would need to reschedule it for the following week. In the meantime she would fax us the brochure for Studio Plus and a letter Roxanne wrote to the baby. I was angry and excited at the same time. Here we had wasted half of the day sitting by the phone. Yet by anticipating the forthcoming letter that helped push those angry feelings aside. My emotions by this time were raw. Trying to sleep at night was pointless. Periodically I found myself on the computer at all hours of the morning and night emailing the other Kelly and praying for this to be over.

A couple days later Sonya called and asked us if we would be willing to come out before the baby was born. The answer was no. We wanted to make sure that Roxanne was still willing to proceed with the adoption plan. We were very well aware that once the baby was born Roxanne would be dealing with many emotions and the last thing she needed was feeling pressured by us or anyone else. The decision for us to fly out to Philadelphia would be left up to her. Roxanne would be the only one that would know when the time was right for us to meet one another and proceed with the adoption plan. At the same time we were not willing to risk flying to Philadelphia and have the adoption plan fall through. I then reminded her we still had not received her fax, containing Roxanne's letter to the baby.

"Very well then," replied Sonya. "I am too busy to fax the information now, but I will do it next week and try to reschedule the conference call."

After not hearing from Sonya for a week I fell back into the tunnel vision mode and became determined to find out how Roxanne was feeling emotionally and physically. I left several messages on Sonya's phone, and emailed her so many times I lost count. Finally I received an email from Sonya stating she had just arrived home.

Subject: Re: Roxanne
Date: Sun, 21 Feb 1999 02"40:42 EST
From: Adoptions1@aol.com
To: Kelly Mostrom

Kelly!!!!!!!!!!! I have your file at my desk for update. I had six girls deliver last week, I was with five of them, when the sixth one went in labor I called the adoptive-mom-to be and told her to get to the hospital. Good and bad move, birth mom discharged forty-eight hours later and adoptive parents took illegal custody of the baby at the hospital and hospital social workers called the police. I have had a crazy week, people flying in weeks before the baby is due. I am assessing girls but ran out of time to type their assessments. I have a social worker to help me with fieldwork; my new assistant just had her baby and I can't wait for her to come back to work. Vivian has not been matched. Will touch base tomorrow, my filing and calling day. I am planning to do the conference call tomorrow between 4:00 p.m. and 6:00 p.m. Roxanne goes to the doctor on Monday. I think they are off by a week or two, but she looks like she can drop at any time. I am preparing the ICPC filing paperwork, consents and custody docs. I have been filing them since an agency inadvertently forgot to file one on one of my clients and ICPC allowed to me follow up and file them. Please confirm from our working agreement that you have payment (s) due. Let me know, then we can discuss. I believe you will be traveling end of February for sure. I have been in the Studio Plus, the Extended Stay, and the Marriott Residence Inn. They are all nice, but the Marriott is nicest…ok I am going to bed. Sonya

Monday meet us with anticipation of the upcoming conference call. Keeping myself busy with work and errands, thoughts of the forthcoming conversations rolled through my head. By 4:00 p.m. I began to pace the floors. By 7:00 p.m. we had not received the phone call. I began calling Sonya's home phone number. We were not surprised that no one answered the phone. Finally I gave up and retired to bed. Angry and confused sleep was the furthest thing from my mind.

The next morning I made several attempts to contact Sonya. After a few hours she finally answered her phone. Anger quickly subsided when she told me Roxanne had gone into labor and that's why there was no call! The baby was born February 23, 1999 at 12:01 EST. He weighed seven pounds, thirteen ounces, and was twenty inches long. His apgars at one minute was nine, and at five minutes was nine point nine. Sonya said he was "a cute baby, with black or dark brown strands of hair and he was a greedy little poop when he ate."

I asked questions like what kind of formula he was on, and if he had been circumcised or not. Questions popped into my head faster then I could get them out of my mouth. How was Roxanne? How were her children? Was there anything she needed?

Sonya told us the baby was on Similac formula, with iron, and that all hospitals circumcise unless they are requested not to. Roxanne was fine but tired and Sonya would check back in with her later in the day.

The next step was to wait seventy-two hours to see if Roxanne would follow through with the adoption plan by signing the relinquishments. If there was any hesitation on Roxanne's part the baby would have to be put in foster care for forty days or until Roxanne was ready to make a decision.

"Roxanne wanted to know if you could fly out in three days, she felt if you were able to come then that she was positive everything would be fine. She also had a counseling session this morning and said she was 100% committed to the adoption plan. She was very removed from the baby and exhibited no maternal instincts. Kelly, I can start the ICPC paperwork if you choose. I have been doing this to help save my clients a few dollars. You would just need to wire transfer $1000.00 and that will take care of consents and the ICPC. Mr. Ginsburg can follow up on the rest but that should save you about $500.00. I will fax you wiring instructions and Roxanne's letter to the baby. Oh, and I need a name for him!" Sonya told me on the phone.

"Kade Levi! And of course we will be there whenever Roxanne wants us to! I will go ahead and make tentative travel plans and after the 72 hours will you call us after she has signed the papers or how will we know when it's safe to fly?" I replied.

"Oh, I like that name Kelly! I will call you at noon on Friday that is when Roxanne is scheduled to sign papers. Ok, I need to go, I will talk to you soon." She said.

The next day, Sonya faxed us Kade's hospital discharge papers and informed us he was in short term cradle care I frantically I made travel plans. Called into work and made tentative arrangements to take twelve weeks off. Then I proceeded to wire Sonya her money, cleaned the house and organized the baby's room. I had to keep myself occupied otherwise I would have gone crazy. Thoughts kept popping in my mind about Deena and what had happened in September. What if we fly out to Philadelphia and Roxanne changed her mind? How would we protect Kassie? I was excited, but not like when we brought Kassie home. This time there was a great deal more anxiety. I couldn't eat, I couldn't sleep and my stomach was always upset. I just had to keep moving to get through the next couple of days.

By Friday morning we were still organizing, packing, and preparing for our trip. And of course, we were waiting for the phone to ring once more.

4

Kade

By noon central time Sonya had not called. Knowing she was ahead of us by one hour I couldn't stand it any longer and called her. Just as I was about hang up Sonya answered her phone out of breath.

"Sonya, this is Kelly, what's happening? We are going insane here!" I exclaimed.

"I just walked in the door, she signed the papers, and you are all set." She replied.

"Sonya, is she sure she wants to proceed with the adoption plan?" I asked.

"Yes, Roxanne said she is 100% sure!" She reported with excitement.

"Okay, we are on our way, and will be there around 3:30 p.m. tomorrow. I will call you when we get checked into Studio Plus." I said enthusiastically.

After we got off the phone Ken and I ran some errands and emailed all of our friends and family to tell them the good news. It was important to us to make Kassie feel included in bringing her new brother home. We stopped at her school and surprised her with a new t-shirt that read, "Finally, I am a big sister", and passed around "It's a Boy" suckers to her class. Ken videotaped the excitement in her face. She was so shocked. It was so cute to see a couple of her little friends jump up and hug her. After we left the school we stopped by the bank to tell my co-workers the news. Finally, after all the errands were done we drove to Ken's parents' house to spend the night. Sonya had suggested that we pick up a small gift for Roxanne. We went to make a quick stop at a store, but it ended up taking hours. We searched for the right gifts. For Sonya we found a silver angel pin with a pearl and a picture frame, we also bought a computer game for her son Marcus as Sonya had mentioned on several occasions how much he liked computer games. After a great deal of contemplating we decided on a gold and diamond necklace for Roxanne. It had three hearts joined together. The hearts symbolized our family, Kade, and Roxanne. We completed our shopping spree by picking out some fun essentials for Kade.

By 6:30 a.m. the next day our plane was taxiing down the runway in Omaha and we were on our way to Philadelphia. I was more nervous than excited. I had an uneasy feeling in the pit of my stomach. Knowing that Roxanne still had forty days to reclaim from the date she signed relinquishments made me uncomfortable and anxious. I had to keep telling myself this was in Gods hands. He doesn't give us what we can't handle. Right?

We stopped in Houston to change planes. On our way through the terminal Kassie spied a stuffed Eeyore doll from the Winnie the Pooh collection. The excitement was apparent so we made a quick purchase and headed to our connecting flight.

We arrived in Philly by late afternoon, rented a car, and headed to Studio Plus. When we were checking in at the hotel, the clerk presented us with a large bouquet of flowers that contained purple iris, daisies, carnations, and small petite roses. They were beautiful and from Kelly and Steve in Wisconsin. Instantly tears came to my eyes. Kelly and I had been through so much together. I knew she was eagerly anticipating the arrival of their baby in a couple of weeks. It was such a lovely gesture and a wonderful surprise.

Our room consisted of a large bed, a sofa hide-a-bed, small kitchenette, a table, and a desk. Immediately I ran to the phone to call Sonya. Her answering machine picked up after several rings. I left a message that we had checked into the hotel and provided her with our room and phone numbers. I was extremely disappointed she was not at home. Sonya knew what time we were arriving so we were afraid to leave the hotel room, just in case she called. The last thing we wanted to do was miss her call. Ken and Kassie went out to find a fast food restaurant, while I continued to wait at the hotel. By the end of the evening we still had not heard from Sonya. After a very restless night I couldn't take it anymore. I called Sonya at 8:00 a.m.

"Hi Kelly, I was just about to call you. I am sorry I didn't get you called last night. I just got out of the shower, and I was at the hospital most of the night, my birth mother Gloria was in labor." Sonya stated.

"Kelly and Steve's birth mom!!!" I exclaimed.

"Yes, wouldn't that be something if both Kelly's were here at the same time!" She said.

"Yes it would! I'll have to call her as I am sure they are so excited." I replied.

"Kelly, I spoke with Roxanne, she wants to bring her other children to say goodbye to the baby and take pictures before she meets you. Mrs. Moore, the social worker that helps me, will be transporting them. When Roxanne is about finished with her goodbyes either myself or Mrs. Moore will call you then you guys can just walk across the street and meet them in the lobby of the Courtyard Marriott." She said.

We needed a car seat for Kade, to take him home on the airplane, so Ken and Kassie ran to Wal-Mart and then was going to stop at Burger King to pick up lunch. When they arrived back at the hotel I was still pacing the floors waiting for the phone to ring. Several hours later I finally broke down at 6:15 p.m. and called Sonya. The phone rang and rang; I knew something had to be wrong. I could feel the anger and anxiety rising in my stomach. A few minutes later the front desk called and said that Sonya Furlow was in the lobby waiting for me. Anxiously I told them to send her back to our room.

After a few minutes of waiting, I couldn't take it; I walked down to the lobby. Sonya was standing at the lobby desk in blue and white hospital scrubs with a light blue hospital cap over her head. She hugged me and said how pretty I was and that my pictures just didn't do me justice.

"You look frumpy in your pictures." She chuckled.

Sonya greeted Kassie with a hug and Ken with a handshake. She pulled out signed and notarized custody papers from her briefcase. As she handed us a copy I noticed our last name was spelled wrong. She quickly made all the corrections by hand and assured us it was not necessary to redo the paperwork.

"It is important you keep these papers close by because you will need them to get Kade on the airplane." Sonya said.

I then explained that we had not heard from Mrs. Moore and I had spent the whole day in the hotel room waiting for the call. Quickly she picked up her cell phone and made a call.

"What's going on?" she asked in a disgusted tone. After moments of silence she said, "I'm on my way."

"I am sorry guys, Roxanne is having second thoughts. Don't worry now, I will go check on her and see what is going on. I will call you as soon as I know something. My pager number is on one of those sheets I just gave you if you need me." She said, halfway out the hotel room door.

Panic struck! We were all numb. Kassie and I were both in tears, as Ken tried to console us. The three of us crawled into bed, huddled together as we laid in shock. Kassie and I said a prayer to God for strength and hope. I kept thinking, why us Lord? I kept repeating to myself that the Lord doesn't give us what we can't handle. Lord, I can't take anymore. Here I am in a strange city, lying on a hotel bed, curled up in a fetal position with my daughter nestled in beside me. Tears were streaming down my face, I could not stop thinking or crying. My mind was racing fifty miles per hour and my stomach was in knots. How could this be happening? Why us? We were all alone miles away from friends and family. I prayed silently, "Oh, Lord, I know you do not give us situations that we cannot handle. I really think I am going to fall apart. Why this? Why? We have been through so much. I cannot do this again. It is too much, please God take the pain away. My heart is breaking into a million pieces. I can't breathe, I can't think. Why?" Suddenly I thought, oh, my God, my daughter!

It was then that I realized I needed to reach down deep inside and pull myself together. We talked with Kassie and explained that no matter how we felt, Roxanne was going through the same emotional turmoil. She had to make a decision on the adoption and one based on what was best for her and her baby. Kassie and I sat down and wrote a letter to Roxanne expressing our thoughts, feelings and support for her. Somehow it helped us both to write her a personal note.

By 11:00 p.m. that evening we still had not heard from Sonya. Ken and Kassie had gone for a ride and picked up an extremely late dinner. I paged Sonya as my stomach was racked with pain. When she returned the call moments later she informed me that she wasn't getting anywhere and she was going to call Tyler and then call us back in the morning. Sleeping was next to impossible. Several times I was up and down. Finally, at dawn, I decided to get up and shower.

Shortly afterwards Sonya called to let us know that she and Mrs. Moore were headed to Roxanne's. When they were finished there she would bring Marcus over to the hotel. I begged Sonya to call as soon as she knew something as I would not leave the hotel room and would be anxiously awaiting her call. Ken and Kassie decided to go for a ride around the area. I sat and flipped through the TV channels motionless, trying to distract myself from the scenarios that were playing over and over in my head.

That afternoon the phone rang. The man on the other end identified himself as Derek Edwards from Adoption Advocates. He said, "I am sorry, Mrs. Mostrom, you have a failed placement."

After that I am not sure what he said. Tears were streaming down my face as I hung up the phone. I was totally caught off guard and baffled by this person calling me. Numb from the emotional roller coaster ride I curled back up on the bed. Just as I began to pull the covers over my head the phone rang again. This time it was Sonya. I told her about someone by the name of Mr. Edwards that had just called and said we had a "failed placement". Sonya became very angry, because it was not his place to make such a call and he had only been helping her out for a short period of time. Too dazed to ask questions I hung up the phone only to have it ring again. It was Mr. Edwards calling to apologize for being so blunt. He recited two phone numbers for us to call if Ken or I needed to talk to someone. I couldn't imagine talking to anyone, let alone a stranger.

Hours later Sonya and Marcus showed up at the hotel. Marcus was a bright-eyed little boy who appeared to be quite taken with Kassie. We gave Sonya and Marcus the gifts we had bought for them and asked Sonya to give Roxanne her gift and the letter Kassie and I had written.

"You don't have to give her that!" She said.

"Yes I do, it was bought for her, and the letter might help her feel better." I replied.

Kassie then grabbed her stuffed Eeyore that we bought at the airport and asked Sonya to give it to Roxanne and the baby. Tears came to my eyes. I was so blessed to have this insightful, kind and giving child.

I sat across from Sonya at the desk in our hotel room. As she spoke to me I had a chill move up my spine. I had not noticed before how pitch black her eyes were. I felt as though she was piercing through my soul. They were so black that I could not see her pupils. I told Sonya we would be changing our plane tickets and would leave Philly earlier than planned. Sonya was emphatic about us getting out of the hotel the next day. She seemed to know that we had not been sightseeing. Frankly that was the furthest thing from our minds and I had no intention of doing so. In my mind, I thought just maybe Roxanne would change her mind tomorrow.

Sonya and Marcus stayed at the hotel for about fifteen to twenty minutes. She needed to check on Kelly Motl's birth mother, Gloria, who had given birth earlier to a little girl. Sonya needed to speak with her about her adoption plan. As they strolled out the door Sonya asked if we wanted to go to dinner the next night around 6:00 p.m. and then we could discuss Roxanne and what the next step would be. We agreed and then they left. Feelings of suspicion and paranoia began to appear that night. I could not get past the gaze of her cold black eyes. Ken and I tried to maintain a happy tone for Kassie's sake. We sat down and mapped out the sightseeing plan for the next day.

The following morning we changed our plane reservations so we could return to Nebraska the next day. I tried to convince Ken to let me stay at the hotel room while him and Kassie went sightseeing. I wasn't in the mood. I felt like I was living in a foggy tunnel and couldn't keep the events from the previous days from replaying in my head. He wouldn't take no for an answer so we went on an historical sightseeing trek.

As we made our way through the city of Philadelphia you could feel the tension amongst us as we forced ourselves to pretend nothing was wrong. We parked the rental car at Penn's Landing and set out on foot. The sun was shining but there a bitter chill as the wind blew between the large buildings. We made our way through the alleys of Franklin Court where Benjamin Franklin had once walked, then through Carpenters Hall and Independence Hall. Our dazed moods had lifted once we reached the Liberty Bell and toured the Betsy Ross House. Kassie was laughing and enjoying herself.

By 3:00 p.m. that afternoon we had returned to the hotel to prepare for our departure the next day. As we packed our bags we realized we still had the new car seat. Ken left for the store to return the car seat, but he arrived back at the hotel very frustrated. The store wouldn't give him cash, only store credit. We decided to box the car seat up and take it back to Nebraska. At 6:00 p.m. our phone rang. It was Sonya. She was talking so fast I had a hard time keeping up. She said she had just spoken with Tyler and he was livid. He had been out of town and just gotten Sonya's messages. Tyler wanted to see Roxanne but Sonya wanted to talk to him first and get him calmed down. She didn't want him going over to Roxanne's by himself, but that would mean we would have to cancel our dinner plans with her. By all means, we weren't worried about our dinner plans. Sonya was concerned about us and wanted to make sure we were eating and sleeping. I reassured her that Ken would go out and bring dinner back to the hotel and I would wait by the phone until she called again.

When Ken was gone Sonya called back. She was at Tyler's and he wanted to make sure we didn't think he was a bad person because he originally had decided to not help Roxanne in any way if she decided to parent the child. I reassured Sonya that we certainly didn't feel that way and wasn't judgmental of either one of them. As the conversation ended Ken walked into the door. I repeated my conversation with Sonya and told Ken that Sonya and Tyler were on their way to Roxanne's.

Suddenly the mood in the hotel room lightened. I couldn't help thinking that maybe this would all work out. Maybe Wal-Mart's refusal to take the car seat back was a sign that we would need it. Speculating became a game as we sat watching television and waiting for the phone to ring. At 11:00 p.m. Ken and Kassie had fallen asleep and a half hour later the phone rang.

"Kelly, I am exhausted. Tyler was really good with Roxanne and just begged her to let you guys take Kade home. He tried to reason with her that it would be best for the baby to have two parents and a stable home life. He even offered to help her get back on her feet financially. Roxanne didn't say much, she just basically listened and said to tell you thank you for the necklace and letter. I set up counseling for her everyday for the rest of this week and for every other day next week. I am sorry Kelly, but this may not be over for awhile." Sonya said.

"Sonya, please tell Tyler thank you." I replied with a lump in my throat.

"Kelly, I will plan on meeting you at the airport tomorrow at 4:30 p.m. You fly out on Continental, right? She asked.

"Yes, we will wait for you at the gate." I stated.

As I hung up the phone the tears started again. Ken reached over to hug and console me. No words were necessary our emotions were overwhelming.

The next day we finished packing, checked out of the hotel, and returned the rental car. When we arrived at the airport we discovered our flight had been cancelled. The desk clerk looked at me like I was crazy as once again the tears started flowing down my face. The last thing I wanted was to be stuck in Philadelphia for another day. We had no car, no hotel, and we were low on cash. My mind began to try to justify the reason the flight was canceled. Was it possible this was a sign? Maybe we were not meant to go home….maybe in a day or two everything would change. Moments later we booked a flight on United Airlines for roughly the same time as our previous flight. I called Sonya and left a message for her to meet us at the United Gate instead of the Continental Gate. We really didn't have a lot of time to spend with her before our flight left and it was important to me that we were able to tell her thank you for everything she had done.

At 4:30 p.m. Sonya had not arrived at the gate so I called her cell phone. She had just pulled into the airport parking garage and would be there shortly. I began to think of the events that had happened while we were in Philadelphia and it dawned on me that when Sonya was in our hotel room we tried to take a picture of her, but she truly didn't want us too. She held up her hands and said how awful she looked and asked that we wait. Sonya had said she hated having people take her picture. The thought crossed my mind that maybe there was a reason that Sonya didn't like to have her picture taken, and if this was a scam of some sort, we needed a photograph. While we were waiting for Sonya, I went to Kassie and showed her how to use the camera and told her that we were going to play a trick on Sonya. Kassie was to wait until Sonya sat down in the airport terminal and then she was to pick up the camera and try to take a couple pictures of her, without Sonya knowing what she was up to. Kassie giggled and thought it was going to be great fun to surprise Sonya with her photography skills.

We watched the terminal and saw Sonya hurrying towards us. As soon as she reached us Kassie gave her a hug. Sonya asked if Kassie had gotten a t-shirt when we were sightseeing. Since she hadn't, Sonya insisted on buying her one. So we walk over to a small shop and Sonya let Kassie pick out a t-shirt of her choice.

Afterwards we sat down in the terminal and Sonya pulled out of her briefcase Tyler's signed notarized consents for the adoption plan, a post card with an address and phone numbers for her new office, and a list of new prospective birth mother situations. Just as she was retrieving the information from her briefcase Kassie called out her name and quickly snapped off two pictures of Sonya. She was definitely surprised and stunned for a moment but then continued explaining the paperwork. Sonya stated she had spoke with Tyler and he tried to contact us that morning but we had already checked out of the hotel. I had told Sonya that I would email her a note for Tyler when we got home and we thanked her for everything she did. Sonya told us the baby had been taken to cradle care and she would call us the following week. The airline called for us to board. I gave Sonya a hug and she wept as she turned to walk away.

The plane ride home was devastating. Too many emotions and too much time to mull over what had just happened in our lives. What would we say to people? How would I be able to remain emotionally calm when answering questions? And then there was work. The very thought of facing my co-workers and the questions they might ask made me sick to my stomach. Upon landing in Nebraska those feelings were only compounded.

Ken was scheduled for surgery in the next few days as he had been diagnosed with sleep apnea. We had stopped at my sister's home in Omaha to pick up a beef we had processed. In our haste to get in the car and drive home I accidentally locked my sisters house keys in her garage. Then to further escalate our emotions we had a flat tire just miles from home. The trunk of the car was filled with frozen meat and bags. As we unloaded the trunk to get to the spare tire Ken and I broke down in laughter. This just had to be a sign. If we could laugh we would get through everything and be just fine.

After a week had passed I called Sonya. A man answered her phone and asked me to call back in ten minutes. I presumed this was her fiancée that she had mentioned on a few occasions. I waited as he had requested and when I tried to call again the phone just rang. No one answered nor did her answering machine pick up.

Later in the evening I tried her number again. This time Sonya answered, I could barely understand her as she was crying hysterically. Sonya said she and her fiancée were in a car accident a few days ago. Her fiancée was driving and the airbag went off. They were fine but he had several lacerations. She had borrowed her mother's car and went shopping. When she returned to the parking lot, the car was gone. It had been stolen and she was panicking because some of her adoption files were in the car. I told her how sorry I was and said I would call her back in the morning.

It took several times the next day to finally reach Sonya. She was in better spirits. They had spotted her mom's car parked in a parking lot near her home. The steering wheel was broken, cash was missing from the glove box, but all the adoption files were there.

Mrs. Moore was coming to pick up Sonya and they were going to visit Roxanne. The baby was doing fine, but he was still in cradle care. Once Sonya spoke with Roxanne she would call or email us with an update. The rest of the day was spent in high anxiety mode. Running around doing errands, and approaching any task with a purposeful determination was my coping mechanism.

By early evening I was helping Kassie get ready for dance class and the phone rang. It was Sonya. My heart jumped as I had a twinge of hope that maybe Roxanne had changed her mind. Sonya reported upon arriving at Roxanne's she was shocked to see that Roxanne had boxed all of her possessions, sold her beds to the neighbors, and was intent on leaving town with a new boyfriend. Roxanne was insisting on $1500 by 9:00 p.m. otherwise she wanted the baby back. I was stunned and angry. Sonya had called Tyler and he was going to send one thousand dollars by Western Union. The rest Sonya was going to take from her son Marcus' piggy bank because she didn't have an ATM card. Mrs. Moore was on her way to pick up Sonya and then they would rush over to Roxanne's, as soon as they knew something she would call us.

I couldn't comprehend what was happening. All of the feelings and emotions came flooding back. I quickly took Kassie to dance and raced back home to sit by the phone. By the time I did return to the house Ken was home from work. He was as shocked as I was. The phone rang and panic struck when I answered as it was Sonya once again.

"Kelly, Roxanne wants the baby back and Mrs. Moore went to go get him out of cradle care." Sonya said in a disgusted tone.

"What can I do? I am shocked!" I replied.

"Well, Roxanne told me $1500 or the baby. I am short $325. Kelly, this guy she is with is a piece of work. He doesn't want the baby or her other kids."

After moments of silence I said, "Sonya, I can lend you the 325 dollars but it needs to be a personal loan to you. I don't want to do anything to jeopardize the adoption and in my state it is illegal to pay a birth mother living expenses."

"Kelly that will be fine. Can you send it Western Union, as soon as possible? I can send you the $325 back in a couple of days, I will call you back as soon as I know something." Sonya replied.

I finished writing down the Western Union instructions. Then immediately called our caseworker, Kay, with our adoption agency. I felt uneasy about wiring the money. Ken and I both felt we better check to make sure we were handling this situation correctly. Kay told us that it would be fine to loan the money to Sonya, but not to pay the birth mother directly. It was a must that Sonya repaid us the $325.00, as we were not allowed to pay birth mother expenses. I gathered my pursed and checkbook and raced to the grocery store to send the money by Western Union and then back home again to wait for Sonya to call. Ken was still on pain medication from his surgery so I called a friend to pick up Kassie from dance class.

At 7:00 p.m. Sonya called back. Mrs. Moore and the baby were in the car waiting. Sonya was on her way to pick up the money I sent. Tyler only had $850 so his new wife was driving down with $225 and Sonya had the rest of the cash. Mrs. Moore was going to drop Sonya off at Roxanne's and then take Kade to Sonya's mother's home. A notary had also been contacted and would meet Sonya at Roxanne's. Sonya was going to insist that Roxanne sign a document stating she was ready to proceed with the adoption plan and a promissory note saying if she changed her mind and later decided against the adoption plan she would owe Sonya the $1500.

So many emotions filled my head. I had spent so many months praying for this yet I felt angry. How could Roxanne use her son as a pawn for money? Before I had so much empathy for her. Trying to decide on whether to complete the adoption plan had to torment her very soul. After speaking with Sonya I was frantic about Roxanne's other children. Sonya had said she was sure they had not been fed and was hoping Roxanne would make an adoption plan for them as well as Kade. The children needed bathing and were not being watched. They were basically left to run the halls of the apartment complex.

I had to email Kelly in Wisconsin; only she would understand the crazy emotions and maybe help me put things in perspective. Only a week before Kelly and Steve found out that their birth mom, Gloria had decided to parent. As I was ready to log on to the computer the phone rang. It was Sonya. Roxanne signed the papers! Once again my emotions soared to an all time high! I needed to share the new developments with Kelly.

Subject: Re: mums the word!
Date: Thu, 11 mar 1999 23:07:24—0600
From: Kelly Mostrom
To: Kelly Motl

Kelly!!

Here's the scoop! Roxanne took the money and evidently signed the necessary papers to proceed with an adoption plan for her all of her children. Now, Ken the one that said, "Only one more child." Thinks we should adopt all of the children! Oh, I don't know! This is scary! Ken was adopted when he was age 7, with a biological sister, age 9, he also had two older brothers and one younger brother but the agency split them up. Ken doesn't want to split the family…of course he is still on medicine from the surgery. I told him Sonya didn't mention us adopting all of them. Ken thinks we may want to let her know tomorrow morning. If Roxanne was to come back I think she would be more likely to reclaim the older children and we would have to look at it as foster care…plus I would have to quit work…not a big deal but it would be extra expense! I called Ken's mom and she said they would help us and would support whatever decision we made. What do we do????????? I have to sleep on this! I am excited but worried about the other three. Talk to you tomorrow!

Kelly

The next morning I was exhausted yet running on adrenaline. Just as I got Kassie out the door to the bus stop, the phone rang.

"Hi Kelly!" said Sonya, with a sound of urgency.

"Hi, what's going on?" I replied.

"I have to make this quick. I have the Department of Health and Human Services on the other line. I just put Roxanne's other children in a foster care home about an hour ago. We couldn't let Roxanne leave last night because she is required by law to have more counseling. The boyfriend left last night as scheduled and after a counseling session this morning she will take a train and meet him in North Dakota."

"So now what?" I asked with hesitation.

"Just hold tight and call me in the morning" Sonya stated.

"I know you are in a hurry, but Ken and I would like to consider adopting all of the children."

"Kelly, I don't know if you want to do that, these kids have lots of issues and are hellions. It would really disrupt your nice family. I need to see what the Department says. I really have to go, I will talk to you later."

As I laid the phone down, my mind started racing. Those poor children, I was sure they were frightened and confused. What a horrifying experience it had to be for them. I myself was having a hard time comprehending the events that had taken place in the last 24 hours. Then I realized we might have to take another trip to the east coast. I scurried around the house in my suit throwing in a load of laundry, picking up papers, and loading the dishwasher. I was having a hard time concentrating as thoughts of Kade and Roxanne flooded my head. I knew I had to clear my thoughts before I got to the bank. I had been working on converting the banks computer system for more than a year and we were less than two months from the conversion date. "Thank God for checklists." I thought to myself. That had been the only way I was able to focus at work and home for months.

Upon arriving at work I made a quick list of things to do just in case I could go pick up Kade. The rest of the day I spent making phone calls and ironing out details of the pending computer conversion that was taking place at work. At times I was excited, then nervous, then angry. With so many emotions I did not know how to handle them other than to force them out of my mind and keep as busy as possible.

That evening Ken and I decided that I would fly to the east coast by myself. We checked flights on the Internet and found it would be cheaper to fly into Baltimore, MD. That would be perfect, as one of my co-workers at the bank had recently moved to Baltimore. Ironically enough, her name was also Kelly. I quickly called to see if she would mind some company. Kelly was a single mom of one little girl and was staying with her mom Pat and her mom's boyfriend, Blair. They were all very excited and assured me they would love to have me as their guest. I was also excited to be able to see them again and to have friends around me during such a monumental moment. I let Kelly know that I would call back as soon as we knew definite plans.

The next morning I called Sonya, she didn't answer so I left a message. An hour later Sonya called back. She was exhausted and loaded down with paperwork. Roxanne did leave on the train to North Dakota and agreed to an adoption plan for all of her children. The following Tuesday Sonya was scheduled to attend an interagency meeting and meet with a judge. The courts usually insist that a sibling group be placed together in one family. Sonya didn't foresee any problems with us bring Kade home since there was an adoption plan previously in place and the other children had not bonded with him.

The older children would be a different story. Sonya needed to contact the birth fathers so it would be questionable as to whether they would even be available for adoption. She received a call from the foster home and the children were crying hysterically. Since she was a licensed foster care home and they knew her she was going to pick them up and let them stay with her. That way she could help calm them down and try to explain to them what was happening. The children knew Sonya, as they often rode with her and Roxanne to doctor's appointments and were use to her visiting them at their apartment.

Ken and I decided one step at a time. Bring Kade home first and if the other children ended up with adoption plans we would do our best to keep the children together. Once again, we were back in the wait and see mode. Waiting and wondering about such a life-altering event was excruciating. With tunnel vision glasses on we went about our daily lives pretending life was normal. Yet deep down inside we were anxious, worried and wondering what the following days would bring.

That evening before going to bed I checked my email as usual. There in front of me was an email from Sonya. Attached to it was a picture of Kade. Finally, I had a picture to go with the name. He laid on a quilt trimmed with red and outfitted in a little white and blue one piece. I studied him for quite sometime. With guilty feelings, for some reason I didn't feel the connection I thought I would. It was hard to really tell what he looked like, as the picture was oversized and a bit fuzzy. He had dark strands of hair, dark eyes, and his little fist was clenched. For some reason, I had thought I would feel an instant connection. I rationalized the feelings by convincing myself it was just a picture, he was cute, he looked like other babies and when I actually held him for the first time I would know he was meant to be my son.

Waiting for the court system took longer than anticipated. Finally, the following Thursday, Sonya called with the good news. We could pick Kade up! The judge had declared that Kade was a separate case from his siblings since an adoption plan had already been in place for several months. The other children would be tied up in the court system until their fathers could be notified. The judge would not waive the 40-day revocation period, but as far as Sonya could tell we had nothing to worry about. Suddenly, I was scared all over again. We had to rethink the situation. Sonya had notified the grandparents and a sister by certified mail that Roxanne was making an adoption plan for the three older children. No one had responded to the notice. Since the paperwork was already in place for

Kade the only thing that could change the adoption was Roxanne returning to Philly to reclaim him.

That evening we spoke with our Pastor and Ken's mom. We were in search of hope and words of wisdom. I had become so use to guarding my heart, and we were scared to death that everything would take a turn for the worse. Sleep didn't come easy that night. Even though Pastor and Ken's mom were encouraging us to make the trip I was still afraid. It wasn't until the next morning when I checked my email that I knew I had to fly to Baltimore.

Immediately, it seemed, I was on a plane to Baltimore with an empty car seat. Kelly was at the airport waiting when I arrived late that evening. It was so fun to see her. Her long dark curly hair was pulled up in a ponytail and she was as excited as I was to see each other again. There was no silence in the car as we made our way through Baltimore to Pat and Blair's home.

I was instantly greeted with hugs and a warm welcome. I had met Pat a couple of times when she flew to Nebraska to visit Kelly. She was a nurse at a local hospital. She was an easygoing person and fun to be around. You could definitely tell they were mother and daughter. They greeted me with gifts for the baby. I was so touched by their thoughtfulness and warm welcome. I called Sonya that evening and left a message that I was in Baltimore.

Saturday morning arrived quickly and there was still no word from Sonya. I called and left another message. At 9:30 a.m. the phone rang, it was Sonya.

"Kelly, I have a dilemma," she said.

"With me??" I replied.

"Yes, I will call you back later." She stated.

The lump in my throat and the instant fear I felt prevented me from asking any questions. My mind went blank and horrible thoughts started to creep into my head. Kelly and I were bound to the house. She tried desperately to reassure and distract me. I spent part of the morning with Kelly showing me how to prepare crab cakes which was a tedious job and a new experience for me. At 1:30 p.m. the phone rang again, and it was Sonya. Speechless I sat and listened in a daze. Roxanne and her new boyfriend were driving down the interstate and he asked her to "perform a sexual act." Upon her refusal he forced Roxanne to perform the act and then "beat the crap out of her and left her along the side of the interstate." The Wisconsin Department of Social Services put her on a Greyhound bus back to Pennsylvania. Roxanne was scheduled to arrive in Lancaster at 6:00 p.m. and Sonya was to pick her up.

With all the hope I could muster I tried to put a bright face on for Kelly. We tried to relieve the tension by going for a ride and stopped to visit her sister.

Upon returning to Kelly's home we proceeded to finish the crab cakes. It seemed like the minutes ticked by so incredibly slowly. It wasn't until 8:30 p.m. when Sonya called again. She was calling from a restaurant near the highway.

Sonya had picked Roxanne up from the bus depot. Roxanne had reassured Sonya she wanted to continue with the adoption plan. With no other place to go, Sonya took Roxanne to her mother's home. Roxanne and her mom had not seen each other for quite sometime. Her mother didn't know Roxanne had already given birth and thought the baby wasn't due until May. Sonya reported that Roxanne's mom sat in a chair with a bible on her lap and said, "We don't give our own away we want the baby back."

I was silent and tears once again rolled down my face. I could hear Sonya crying amongst all the noise in the background.

"Kelly, I am so sorry, I feel like I just broke your heart in millions of pieces." Sonya said as she was blubbering.

"Yes, it feels that way." I said with tears rolling.

"I will make finding you a baby my first priority." She retorted.

After another sorrowful sleepless night I flew back to Nebraska. Kelly and her family were kind enough to keep the car seat for me. They would box it up and send it UPS. Kade was not meant to be our son. The journey home was a long and tearful one. I sat on the plane in a daze preparing myself as to what I would tell our family and friends, once again.

5

Justice?

After returning home from Baltimore, the woman named Sonya Furlow sent the world crashing down on my shoulders. Thinking back to the times I felt guilty for calling Sonya so many times, to her hugging Kassie, and us feeling sorry for her for being so overworked now made my stomach turn.

After setting up a fake email box under the name of Jan Monson I responded to a post on the fertilethoughts.net board. A "Cheri" was asking questions about Sonya Furlow. I wanted to know why she was asking, as I had my own suspicions but wasn't ready to accept them. Cheri wrote back and left a phone number and said "please call Rex, we are conducting inquiries into Sonya Furlow." I didn't respond. Why? I was afraid, and rightfully so. A few days later our attorney from Philadelphia, Jay Ginsburg, called.

He was very careful and didn't want a defamation of character suit against him. He had been contacted by a private investigator hired by one of his clients. The private investigator asked Jay to contact all of his clients that had a working relationship with Sonya Furlow to see if we would call and talk to him. At this point Jay was still uncertain whether Sonya was legit, or if she was just over-worked and sloppy. Jay did have a client that had received a baby through Sonya in December and the adoption was close to being finalized.

I called the private investigator. My first impression was that he was arrogant, rude, and gruff. How could I trust him? I told him who I was and he simply responded "yeah."

I said, "I am calling about Sonya Furlow."

"I have been told not to talk to you because you will go back and tell Sonya." He said sarcastically.

I became very angry and yelled, "Why in the hell would I do that? If she has screwed me over I want her ass nailed to the wall!"

"Oh, I didn't think people in Nebraska talked that way." He chuckled, but it was no laughing matter. The last year of my life had begun to unravel.

After making the phone call to Rex and some preliminary investigations our worst fears were confirmed. We had been scammed. There were never any babies, no birth moms, and all the stories Sonya told us were completely fabricated. The investigation started with 10 couples that used the same prominent attorney.

In a crazed frenzy I made massive phone calls to attorneys, the FBI, the local police department, and the states attorney generals offices. We didn't know what to do with ourselves emotionally, or how or who to contact to make sure Sonya was stopped. It was difficult to determine whom we could trust. I had to make sure someone would follow through.

Then it occurred to me that Adoption Visions had mentioned in the last couple of months that they had stopped doing business with Sonya in September of the previous year. Why were we not told then? After all, the contract was between Sonya Furlow, Adoption Visions, and us. They assured me Sonya had been thoroughly checked out and they were confident she would be clean. I sent more profiles to them in an act of desperation hoping our child would be found soon.

Our evenings were spent printing copies of all my emails and gathering documents given to us by Sonya. By the time I was done compiling my evidence I had a stack of emails and other information four inches thick. I had located receipts from Western Union, letters, and envelopes from Sonya. All along I had a feeling or a voice talking to me, telling me something didn't feel right. I just could not decipher it. I was just too vulnerable or desperate, so much so that I kept rationalizing and reading into the situations what I wanted to believe.

Regardless, the banker side in me was smart enough to keep copies of everything. With every emotion I had left I had to do the only thing I could. That was to fight back. "Lord," I begged, "have mercy and forgive me but I must do everything in my power to shut down Sonya and Adoption Visions so they cannot continue destroying peoples lives."

I was embarrassed and ashamed that we had been duped. Each interview with the police and the FBI made me tearful and heartbroken all over again. As their investigation progressed we played the game with Sonya and Adoption Visions for a short time until finally demanding our money back. As time moved forward eventually the shock wore off and more anger began to develop. I stayed in contact with Sonya until she finally returned the 325 dollars she borrowed. On the day that our bank did their computer conversion the FBI walked into my office. It was like a clip from a movie. One was about 6'5" with a military haircut, and the other was about 5'10" and reminded me of a computer analyst. They were dressed casually; they then removed their sunglasses and flashed their badges. The interview lasted for a couple of hours. I felt relief as now I had someone to contact whom I could trust to keep me posted on the proceedings in Philadelphia. It soon became an inside joke with those closest to us as I referred to them as my "little FBI men." Humor was still hard to find.

As the rest of 1999 moved on we found ourselves in pursuit of our child. The summer was spent sending out mass mailings and letting everyone know that we wanted to adopt a child. It was then that we realized the grieving process had begun.

Daily I maintained contact with Kelly Motl in Wisconsin, trying to keep abreast of the investigation of Sonya's case and discussing our quest to get a refund from Adoption Visions. It became apparent that the FBI did not have a case against Adoption Visions. Was it possible they were victims or just had sloppy business practices?

Throughout this time period, on the Internet, we began to meet other couples that were victims of Sonya. Sharing our stories helped the healing. The grief process was a long and hard one as closure to me was to complete our family and then to see justice for all involved.

I started to journal my feelings. It seemed that the people closest to me didn't understand what I was going through. The only way I could describe this unfathomable experience was that we greatly anticipated the arrival of a child after waiting many years; only instead, we had to experience the grieving process as though the children had died. To make matters worse was the fact we had found out that those we waited for and grieved over didn't even exist. I came to the conclusion that no one truly understands a life-altering event such as our experience, a death, or an illness, unless they have personally been through it. People can have empathy, but they cannot truly understand it.

The private investigator, FBI, and local police had in their possession all of my personal intimate emails written over the last year. After having our hearts ripped out of our chests twice and then learning we had been scammed, kept it hurting all over again. I felt myself falling into a deep tunnel of depression. I would claw my way up the wall only to slide back down. For months I wasn't obsessed with getting even. It was more a feeling of why me? Why us? Was this God's plan? How did I get to this point of despair? Some days were better than others. I was so focused on the adoption and lost track of my other priorities. It was during this time I met my mentor, Ellen Roseman.

Ms. Roseman was a "working facilitator" and adoption advocate who had been working with adoptions in California for over twenty years. She had an impressive background. She was the California Representative for the American Adoption Congress, on the Board of Directors for Resolve of Northern California, and an active member of The California Adoption Alliance, The Coalition for Adoption Reform and Education, The National Open Adoption Coalition, The Council for Equal Rights in Adoption and many other organizations I was unfamiliar with at the time. I discovered that she also presented adoption related workshops across the country and was well know as someone who was passionate about children's rights and openness in adoption. Through Ellen I learned to educate myself, process, read, write, listen and process some more. By doing this I was able to empower myself and learned quickly that I had been living in a box. There was much more to the adoption world and I found myself not as informed or educated about adoption as I had previously thought. Through her guidance and instruction I was able to move forward.

On April 11, 2000, the United States Attorney Michael Stiles distributed a press release. It "announced the filing of an indictment against Sonya Furlow, charging Furlow with 20 counts of mail fraud, arising from an extensive adoption fraud scheme, in which Furlow matched prospective adoptive parents with fictitious birth mothers, only to later inform them that the adoptions had failed. Furlow gained approximately $215,000 from this fraud." (Stiles, 2000)

The press release also revealed that the indictment charged, "that between January 1997 and December 1999, Furlow used the Internet to establish contact with prospective adoptive parents and to advertise her services as an 'adoption facilitator' who could assist in the adoption process by locating and matching birth mothers who intended to" make an adoption plan. "Furlow informed prospective adoptive parents that she operated an adoption facilitation service known as Tender Hearts Family Services" at two separate addresses in Philadelphia, Pennsylvania. Furlow further represented that she had contact with numerous birth mothers who intended to make adoption plans for their children.

Additional information from the April 11, 2000 press release stated that, "in Pennsylvania, individuals were permitted to act as 'facilitators' in the adoption process primarily by locating and matching birth mothers who intended to" make an adoption plan for their children "with prospective adoptive parents, but facilitators were not licensed and could not finalize an adoption. The termination of parental rights could only be effectuated through an attorney, and an attorney or a licensed agency was required to file the paperwork associated with an interstate adoption." (Stiles, 2000)

The following excerpt from the press release concluded: "between January 1997 and December 1999 Furlow informed approximately 44 sets of prospective adoptive parents that they had been matched with fictitious birth mothers, or in a few cases, with persons who existed but were not pregnant or did not intend to put their babies up for adoption. Furlow required the prospective adoptive parents to pay substantial up front fees, ranging from $1,000 to $15,000, upon being matched with a birth mother, demanding and receiving approximately $215,000 from the 44 sets of prospective adoptive parents.

Furlow used various means to create the impression that the fraudulent matches were legitimate. For example, Furlow provided photographs of alleged birth mothers, which in reality were photographs of other prospective parents and/or their friends and relatives that had been sent to Furlow as part of their adoptive parent packages. Furlow sent or directed others to send email messages, which were allegedly from the fictitious birth mothers. Furlow also had third persons pretend to be fictitious birth mothers during conference calls with the adoptive families. In some instances, Furlow provided falsified medical records relating to a fictitious birth mother or baby. Furlow told most of the adoptive parents that the fictitious birth mothers did not want to meet them, thereby deflecting request for face-to-face meetings.

Furlow eventually informed the prospective adoptive parents that the adoptions had failed, citing a number of reasons for the failure, including a change of mind by the birth mother or father, the reappearance of the previously disinterested birth father or ex spouse, interference by the birth parents' families, or illness or problems with the birth mother or newborn. Furlow frequently informed the prospective adoptive parents that the birth parents had decided to place the child with another family due to an alleged inadequacy on the part of the adoptive family, such as a physical impairment, their religious affiliation, inability to pay additional money for the adoption, or lack of adequate financial support during the pregnancy. Furlow also told clients that requested to meet with or have more access to fictitious birth mothers that they were too pushy and had alienated the birth mother by their demands.

Furlow also directed several families to travel from distant locations, such as Utah, and Kansas, to Philadelphia to pick up babies that did not exist, and once they arrived, would inform that problems had developed. Furlow told many of these families that the adoptions would likely go through despite the last minute problems, causing them to stay at hotels in the Philadelphia area for several days and even weeks waiting for the adoption papers to be signed or the problems to be resolved.

Many of the 44 sets of prospective adoptive parents were rematched with another fictitious birth mother or mothers upon the failure of the first match, or were promised an additional match which never materialized. Although many families ultimately demanded a refund, Sonya Furlow only refunded money to three of the families, and only one of those families received a full refund." (Stiles, 2000)

Special Agent Darin Werkmeister of the FBI, and Postal Inspector Anthony Wolchasty of the U.S. Postal Inspection Service investigated the case. The case had been assigned to Assistant United States Attorney Bernadette McKeon. (Stiles, 2000)

In June of 2000 Furlow plead guilty to three counts of mail fraud. (The E.D. of Pa., 2000) One count was for Ken and I. We were somewhat relieved, yet it was appalling that the only crime she could be charged with was mail fraud. During the next several months we were busy completing our family, and during that same time frame we were subpoenaed to attend the sentencing, prepared a victim impact statement, and continued to pursue Adoption Visions for a refund.

At 9:30 am on September 8, 2000, we found ourselves seated in the United States District Court, Eastern District of Pennsylvania, directly behind Sonya Furlow, to our left was Kelly and Steve Motl. The Honorable Eduardo C. Robreno was presiding and the court was packed with other victims. It was apparent Sonya had gained a lot of weight over the year. She sat motionless and emotionless throughout the proceeding while five victims testified at the hearing, describing the loss of trust, emotional trauma, and loss of money. Sonya addressed the court, blaming her actions on drug abuse and mental illness. To me she appeared to be going through the motions of court, I saw no remorse and a lack of emotion as she spoke.

As we sat behind Furlow in court I found myself feeling reflective. I had so many feelings, anger, hurt, sorrow, and relief. How could she have hurt so many families emotionally for her own financial gain? I kept reminding myself that Sonya was a con artist and a very good one at that. A con doesn't have a conscience so it makes it hard for others to see they are lying. I hoped one day she would see what she did was wrong, but it was not up to me to judge. Someday she would meet her Maker and He would be the one to pass down judgment. In a strange way I felt sorry for her.

At times I had thought of her as a friend. Those detrimental thoughts made me question my judgment to trust in my co-workers and friends. I was always the people pleaser, the person who fully trusted others and always cheered for the underdog. The trust and my self-confidence would take a great deal of time to be restored. My focus needed to be on regaining control of my life. Throughout the trial I replayed in my head "God doesn't give us what we can't handle." I knew I would be stronger after this experience.

On September 9, 2000, The Philadelphia Inquirer printed an article entitled "4-Year Term in Adoption Swindle", written by Joseph A. Slobodzian, an Inquirer staff writer. The article quoted U.S. District Judge Robreno as saying, "The string was played out. You played on one of the most basic human needs and instincts—to have a child and raise a family." Slobodzian reported Judge Robreno, noted "the emotional devastation she had caused, said Furlow had remained in contact with victims even after she received money and the adoption had failed." Furthermore, Robreno stated Furlow's conduct was "particularly and unusually cruel." (Slobodzian, 2000)

My most vivid memories of the court room and Judge Robreno were the fact that he eluded to the limits imposed on him by the federal sentencing guidelines and if he was able he would have imposed a harsher sentence. It was clear as the proceedings progressed that the federal sentencing guidelines were so rigid that they gave no latitude for Judge Roberno's discretion. Roberno's poignant last few words to Furlow were that this was "the cruelest con," the chilling echo of the judge's last words would always remain with me. He then ordered Sonya Furlow to pay $215,000 in restitution and sentenced her to 3 years and 10 months in prison with no parole, followed by three years of supervised release.

As we walked out of the courthouse we were met by a flurry of reporters. It truly was a scene for a movie as the Motl's, Ken and I scurried together through the reporters with cameras in our faces and the popping off of several questions simultaneously. We grabbed the closest taxi and once the door opened you could feel everyone being pushed from behind. As the door shut on the taxi I remember Steve Motl as saying "lets get the hell out of here!"

After the sentencing we met for lunch with some of Sonya's other victims. It was clear there was some sense of relief yet plenty of disappointment for the short prison term. All of the victims had devastating stories and several of them worse then our own story. By all accounts Sonya reportedly was financially broke so it was unlikely the victims would see any compensation. If they did it would be only a small fraction of what was ordered. It was surreal to finally be around others that knew your feelings and shared the common bond, even though that bond was being a victim of Sonya Furlow.

Periodically throughout the next few years I would find myself with new questions and at times attempting to reanalyze the Furlow fiasco. In search of more answers I contacted Jay Ginsburg. I was curious as to how Sonya's scheme was uncovered. Through a telephone interview on July 21, 2003, Mr. Ginsburg explained that he had received a phone call from a couple in Colorado asking if he was handling their adoption.

Mr. Ginsburg reported, "I had never heard of him before."

The caller gave Mr. Ginsburg a brief run down of their adoption scenario.

Mr. Ginsburg reportedly said, "wait a second I just heard the same story from somebody else here in Pennsylvania that I am doing an adoption for. Would you like to talk to her? Something is not right here."

Being cautious about not jumping to conclusions, Mr. Ginsburg confided that he thought it was a possibility that maybe Sonya accidentally duplicated efforts on one family, yet it made him nervous. Mr. Ginsburg then contacted his other client in Pennsylvania to get her permission to have the Colorado couple call her and compare stories. From that point the private investigator was brought into the picture and Mr. Ginsburg began to work with him in developing a timeline.

During the phone interview I asked Mr. Ginsburg what his reaction was and what his thoughts were on Sonya.

He replied, "We are all middle class people. We were all raised to believe that people tell the truth; you believe in God, you believe that when people give their word it means something. It was all a tremendous shock to me. The whole thing was so remarkable to me in the complexity of the scheme, and yet it was so straightforward in many ways. Honest people expect honesty from other people. People that are looking to raise a family are usually absolutely doing it for the right reasons. To me, just having a family is the most important thing you could do in life. Anyone can be fooled. Some people will always prey on decent people."

It was clear during this interview that in the beginning Mr. Ginsburg did not have a reason to doubt Sonya. An adoptive family that was working with Sonya contacted him to help complete their adoption. According to Mr. Ginsburg, he finalized the successful adoption for twins in May 1999.

"Sonya did a good job and the adoption went extremely well, she really knew what she was doing." He said.

In order for a scam of this magnitude to work, Sonya had to first set up and complete at least one successful adoption, before she could move forward. Typically most scam artists, in whatever scam they are trying to pull off, have to some how establish some kind of credibility before they implement their schemes.

In my conversation with Mr. Ginsburg, he took a great deal of time explaining Pennsylvania's adoption law. It was clear that the laws were very complicated. Sonya had explained the basics to us yet there was much more to them.

Mr. Ginsburg also stated that, "At the time of these events, Pennsylvania was probably one of the states in which it took the longest to terminate parental rights, which is why people often would go out of state." In a letter from Mr. Ginsburg dated January 25, 2005, he stated "Upon until the revisions in the

Pennsylvania Adoption Statue in May 2004, in a consensual adoption the birth parent could revoke anytime up until the moment when the Judge signed the final decree to terminate their rights."

Those statements just confirmed my theory, which was Pennsylvania's adoption law made it conducive or easy for Sonya to pull off her scam. Effectively, the laws gave her plenty of time to come up with more excuses as to why the adoptions were on hold or had failed. Thankfully, Mr. Ginsburg had the insight and instinct to see the red flags that were brought before him and took steps to help bring an end to Sonya's con.

After the trial had come to an end, I was still seeking justice for the shoddy or in my opinion unethical practices of the California facilitator who originally matched us with Sonya Furlow. The FBI had cleared Adoption Visions out of Berkeley, CA of any illegal violations or direct connection with Sonya, showing they were not running the con together. Yet in my mind they certainly were on the borderline of being unethical and operating their business in the gray area of California's adoption law. If nothing else I felt they needed to accept some kind of responsibility. After all, they knew something was wrong months before Sonya's scam was uncovered, as they had quit working with her and failed to inform the rest of their clients until the news about Sonya broke.

As November rolled around I found myself embroiled in a letter writing campaign to Nebraska's Governor, the Attorney Generals in Nebraska and California, the Better Business Bureau and I was filing complaints online as I was in pursuit of a refund from Adoption Visions. Eventually we were offered a refund of $1,500 provided we sign a specific release stated below:

"AV and the Family hereby agree to immediately and permanently discontinue and communications, postings, or disseminations of information of any kind regarding the other party. Specifically, the family will discontinue presenting information, whether the family deems such information to be true and correct or not, on any and all message boards, Internet services, or in writing or verbally to any party whatsoever. In plan language, the Family will <u>walk away</u>. Both parties will agree that whereas they both had the best of intention in working with each other, the relationship did not work out by no fault of either party. Any action inconsistent to this agreement by either part will be a violation of this agreement and may be considered slander, libel, interference with the others business, or any other tort will be subject to civil action for monetary damages." (Adoption Visions, 2000)

There was no way in hell we were going to sign any such thing! I had made several attempts to get them to file a claim with their bonding company or provide me with information on their insurance agent and their bond. On several occasions they stated they had spoke to their insurance agent, attorney and had brought the matter before their board of directors for the corporation. According to Adoptions Visions, all parties involved felt we had no claim. However, I discovered that according to California Family Code, they were in violation of specific sections. And in our contract it specifically stated that Adoption Visions would obtain proof of pregnancy, have comprehensive interaction with birth mother to determine commitment level, and they would obtain background information on the birth mother. Perhaps, if they actually followed that code they would have known that the birth mothers did not exist.

It was obvious to me that, at minimum, they had poor business and personal ethics, wrote contracts, collected the cash and would move on to the next client, perhaps if they had obtained the necessary documentation we might have had a chance of avoiding this entire fiasco. Furthermore, the $2000 paid to Adoption Visions was only to be paid upon a match with a specific birth mother. How could the contract be valid when there were no "real" birth mothers?

As the months went by I realized we were getting nowhere with Adoption Visions. I began talking with others through email and researching the bonding companies only to discover from Ellen Roseman there was only one company that bonded most, if not all of the facilitators, at the time, in California. I called the headquarters for the insurance company on the east coast and told them I wanted to file a claim against Adoption Visions. On March 8, 2001, when the bonding company finished their investigation, we received a check for a partial refund in the mail. Certainly it did not cover all of our expenses but it was, at that time, more the principal of the idea then the money.

I was eager to share my information with Kelly Motl and other victims. Unfortunately, after further research we discovered the bond was for exactly $10,000, the amount required by California law. That meant the bonding company would only pay out a total of ten thousand dollars, not $10,000 for each client that was victimized. Kelly Motl and the other victims involved with Adoption Visions would only able to collect on the remaining amount of the bond. The plus side to filing the claim against the bonding company was that Adoption Visions was driven out of business. I assumed it was highly unlikely they would ever be bondable and without that bond they could not operate in the State of California.

Finally, I had some sense of relief. It was only the end of a chapter but not the end of the book. Emotionally, I was still devastated. My time had to be redirected to focus on my family and the healing process.

PART II
The Journey's Aftermath

6

Moving On

Explaining the devastation, hurt and grief, we felt was extremely difficult. Society is not educated sufficiently enough about adoption itself, let alone the grief someone experiences over a child who has been relinquished by a birth parent, reclaimed by a birth parent, or over a failed adoption plan of any kind. Our anticipation led our minds to create images of our child. Even though the children did not exist, in our hearts and minds they were very real.

Without a strong support group it was extremely difficult to work through the grief. Still, in our hearts those babies existed. Maybe they were fabrications, but over months they became the fulfillment of our dreams. After the Furlow story broke our grief was so intense that we were lost as to how to handle it. Friends and family tried to listen, to support us, and attempted to understand our situation. Yet, it was very hard for them to understand or empathize for a situation they had never experienced. I relate it to someone who has a life threatening illness. I can try to understand and support them although I don't really comprehend their situation fully as I have never had to experience such a life-altering event. I searched for a Nebraska RESOLVE Support Group, only to discover there was not one. But I was still able to join the National RESOLVE Organization where I was able to draw on some of their resources and educational information.

I was lost, floundering for words, trying to comprehend and searching for someone to blame. I blamed myself and was overcome with grief and guilt. Continually I searched for reasons why. How could it be I was grieving for a child who never existed? Later I learned from Ms. Roseman that paradox in adoption is common and this was only one of many. Just as I grieved for a child that didn't exist on the other end of the spectrum birth mothers in an open adoption grieve for a child who is alive and healthy.

During my grieving process I felt as though I had lost my dream, my child and my perception of the positive adoption experience had been shattered. My support group dwindled; friends had heard enough and couldn't comprehend the devastation this experience had on me. Slowly, I sank into the dark tunnel of depression, occasionally grasping at straws to pull me up only to slide further back into the tunnel. Why? I just wanted to know 'Why me'? Then I realized, it just wasn't me, there were many adoptive families that got scammed. But what did I miss and what made me a target? For one thing I stepped outside of my box, by using someone other then our original adoption agency without being totally educated and informed. I had made assumptions and had a preconceived notion that our second adoption would work and turn out just as perfect as the first. I always prided myself on choosing friends that were of good character and on making good business decisions. Suddenly, I had to reevaluate myself and learn to trust my decisions and instincts all over again.

My coping skills in this life-altering event were limited, to say the least. To avoid questions I began to isolate myself. When I couldn't, I found my heart racing and felt sick to my stomach when faced with public appearances. Soon I experienced flashbacks of Sonya looking at me laughing on the telephone. I was overwhelmed by my own inadequacies, by my lack of trust in others and in my own ability to make good decisions. I was stuck in the role of a victim and did not know how to get out. Time passed quickly yet the same scenes continued to replay in my head in slow motion. Through the normal grieving process I found myself becoming more resilient and stronger as each day passed. Resilience is and can be developed and you may not recognize it at the time. Looking back at situations and analyzing them often give people new and positive insights.

I was a strong woman, always on time when something needed done. Nothing was left on the back burner. Fairness, integrity, and justice were the values I lived by. My philosophy was always to cheer on the underdog in any situation, just give them a chance. Suddenly, I was the underdog scratching my way to the top of the tunnel only to have my own inadequacies, thoughts, and feelings knock me back down. I didn't know what to do, or how to fix it.

Finally, I broke down and sought professional help. In my mind I had always believed it was a sign of weakness if you had to ask for help. No longer do I feel this way. I used my inner courage and strength to find someone to help me out of the tunnel of darkness and because of that I quickly learned I was in charge of my life. Yes, someone had shit on me and it was terrible. But I had to get my life on track and then do something to help others.

When there is a death in the family you have rituals that help heal and lead to closure. In this situation Sonya's sentencing was as close to closure as I would ever get. The years of focusing on my career and the pursuit of completing my family left me drained and I found myself neglecting me and unsure of how or when to refill my cup. I didn't even know what I needed to feel better. The healing process could have been much faster if I had paid attention to my needs and just taken the shit out of my pocket and moved on.

Each person experiences grief differently so we all have to experience the cycle on our own timeline. I first experienced the shock and denial, then isolation, bargaining, anger, despair, and finally resolution. Sometimes my feelings overlapped or reverted back through the earlier multiple stages of grief. Somehow, I had to gain the mindset of a survivor. But before I did that I would occasionally fall back into the victim role and have to consciously pull myself back out of the darkness by my bootstraps.

Taking care of myself was the key. I first had to learn what that meant: take time out to read, go for a walk, work in the yard, sit in the sun and reflect on the beauty of nature and the gifts God gave me. Focusing on the positive was a chore, but the positive thoughts were what brought to me to the other side.

According to Pat Johnston and Wendy Williams in their article entitled "Losing an Adoption: Practical Advice for Moving on After a Uniquely Painful Experience." "Parents who have suffered adoption reversals express frustration at the attempts of professionals and caring others to comfort them by suggesting that this loss is like some other, more commonly experienced parenting loss." (Johnston, Williams, 2003) To elaborate further I believe this spectrum can be broadened to include people involved in adoption scams and any member of the adoption triad that has suffered through a loss during the adoption process. At some point if you are involved in an adoption scam be aware that grief can encapsulate you. Its important to understand that you are not alone and recognize the necessary steps needed move on.

I struggled to find comfort in others. My saving grace was being able to speak with other victims of Sonya Furlow. It was reassuring and comforting to know they had the same feelings, were searching for someone to blame, and were trying to regain control of their lives. Johnston and Williams also suggest that great comfort can be found in finding others that have had the same or a similar experience because often times there can be no closure. The child, if it existed, may be growing up in a home somewhere else, with another name and family. Johnston and Williams also state in their article, "Losing an Adoption: Practical Advice for Moving on after a Uniquely Painful Experience", that "Parents will continue to be aware of the milestones as time progresses. It will hurt less as time goes by, but one will not forget or lose any of the intensity of the love felt for a child."(Johnston, Williams, 2003) I myself had to recognize the grief, acknowledge the love and loss then decide to move on. It was not easy. I had good days and bad days. Continually I had to reevaluate myself and make the decision to move on. Thinking positive, trying to look at the situation as a learning experience, and realizing that I was a victim but needed to step over to the other side kept me from becoming bitter and stuck in the victim role. I am not saying that I wasn't bitter and resentful at times, but each day I had to focus on moving forward and letting go. During this time it is important to take care of yourself.

Jane Ryan, in her most recent book "Broken Spirits~Lost Souls Loving Children with Attachment and Bonding Difficulties" offers the following as Basic Guidelines for Self Care:

1. Eat, sleep, and don't forget the basics in life

2. Take some time for yourself each day to read, rest, daydream and play.

3. Stay in contact with others by phone or in person.

4. Tell the truth of your experience and share your deepest feelings.

5. Seek out a support group or others that have had a similar experience.

6. Actively seek out appropriate professionals for therapy and support.

7. Spend time with your spouse and make time for special activities with your other children or family members.

8. Laugh and pray for the children, parents and all involved. (Ryan, 2002)

It was necessary for me to take time off of work when I learned of the "failed adoption plans". There was no way I could function and desperately needed that time to sort through my feelings and relive the experience by talking to my husband and other family members. I had a close friend call other friends and explain the situation. By having her field those initial comments of shock and disbelief gave me the opportunity to formulate a response to questions that would predictably follow such losses. I knew it would be difficult to talk to others without showing the raw emotions. Yet I felt better knowing how and what I would say when questions were asked.

Often times, hugs and quiet moments among family members helped ease the pain. Moving myself from the isolation and safety of my home proved to be the real challenge. Feelings of guilt, despair, and embarrassment often flooded my every movement in the outside world. I actively had to seek out friends that acknowledged and validated my feelings and grief, while distancing myself those that didn't understand or were ignorant of adoption or my situation. When friends weren't available I turned to my journal and emailed the other victims of Sonya. Eventually I began to believe in the positive self-talk and constantly reminded myself that what doesn't kill you will make you stronger. It took awhile because just like learning from your mistakes, everyone must heal and grieve at each individual's own pace.

There is no timeline for healing and moving on. Being compassionate and understanding with those around you who don't always understand your situation is hard, so you must afford them God's grace. This was not the time to dwell on negative comments or focus on life-altering decisions. It was a time to reevaluate myself, the true me, and my self worth.

When the time was right, and doing it in small steps, I eventually cleaned out the nursery. I packed the special items and stored them away and gave the rest to charity and friends. I did not want any reminders of the child that wasn't meant to be ours. I couldn't bear using any of the clothes or trinkets for another child. Slowly I found the proper place for everything in the nursery. This helped with closure and was a relief, rather than a constant reminder every time I walked past the nursery.

Recovering from an emotional loss takes time and a conscious effort to move forward. When the depression or sadness is overwhelming you must force yourself to reflect and look forward. Taking a small shopping excursion while avoiding the baby section or any reminders of the child you lost can be very therapeutic. Even small weekend get-a-ways were helpful although, upon returning home the same thoughts and feelings would sometimes return. Gradually life got easier.

However, I was unprepared for the return of these emotions and hurt when we decided to try to adopt again. Some of the joy of our adoption was clouded by these emotions. The sense of loss and the loss of trust piled up a barrier inside; a barrier was put in place to guard my heart. It was then, at that time a natural response to want to protect myself from the hurt. Upon trying to adopt again all the memories from the previous experiences came flooding back. The key was to put both experiences in perspective and learn from previous mistakes. Each adoption was different in its own right. I couldn't allow guilty feelings to creep into our new adoption. Some of the joy was gone as a result of our experiences with Sonya Furlow. We knew life would not be the same after such events. We were more cautious, skeptical and guarded.

It was at this time we began to incorporate rituals into our lives to celebrate our new adoption. Rituals can be healing and will make your new adoption special while putting more closure on the past adoption loss. Life does return to normal and eventually you do begin to heal. Laughter and joy will return. The memories will not be forgotten, but that is okay, new happier times will follow.

Ellen Roseman, an educator and advocate for open adoptions, in an article entitled, "Rituals and Ceremonies in Celebration of Adoption" states, "Rituals can provide a meaningful bridge out of secrecy and shame which have been prevalent in traditional adoptions of the past. We know children learn more from what we feel than what we say. Rituals celebrated with openness, love, and pride send a powerful message of validation to those around us and most importantly, to the infant or child entering our family. Pre-adoption rituals and post adoption family rituals, whether they are complex or simple, contribute to family connections and integration. Rituals acknowledge feelings, define relationships, and mark transition in our lives."(Roseman, 2000)

As an adoptive mom of the early 90's I could honestly say I could not see the benefits of an open adoption. Now as an adoptive mom of the 21st century, I believe open adoption is beneficial for all members of the adoption triad. In my own mind I had come to the decision that neither the birth mother nor the adoptive parents are a threat to each other, rather they are working toward one goal, which is bonding together as a family for what is in the best interest of the child. Often the adoptive parents may fear the unknown. It's the fear and the search of entitlement they may be seeking. Perhaps if we had requested a complete open adoption and forced this issue with Sonya Furlow we may have be able to avoid or at the minimum, stop the process before we became so deeply involved in her scam.

Of course, the circumstances of an adoption depend on the degree of openness. Certainly in cases of abuse or neglect the openness should be considered carefully. It always comes back to the same question. What is in the best interest of the child? Nevertheless, rituals in an open adoption, or a failed adoption can be therapeutic and can validate and soothe feelings.

Certainly one of the worse tragedies a family can experience is the death of a child. At the time we considered our impending adoptions, as failed adoptions even though we later learned the children and birth mothers didn't exist. In our minds they were very real. Consequently, we had to grieve as though we had lost a child.

One way to acknowledge the failed adoption, the child or your grief is by lighting a candle in a private ceremony in remembrance of the child you lost; this could be done on his or her birthday. In the article, "Rituals and Ceremonies in Celebration of Adoption by Ellen Roseman, she discusses the original candle ceremony that was used at the NACAC (North American Council on Adoptable

Children) Conference in California in 1999. The ceremony is celebrated on a finalization date or the child's birthday. It entails the lighting of five candles: the first honors and remembers the birth family, the second honors adopted children and adults, the third is in honor of adoptive parents, the fourth honors those waiting to be parents, and the fifth candle is lit in honor for children awaiting adoption. This candle ceremony was "initially developed by Robin Byrnes and celebrated...during Adoption Week in 1994." (Roseman, 2000)

Ms. Roseman also explains in her article that many times in open adoptions entrustment ceremonies are held where the birth family and adoptive family come together to honor "the child moving permanently from one family to another."(Roseman, 2000) The ceremonies can be held in a church, chapel, home, or hospital. Ms. Roseman states, "this ceremony is one in which losses and gains, joy and sadness, and the present and future are acknowledged and embraced." Each participant can offer a promise or wish to the cherished child as a way to mark the transition. "It gives new meaning to the term: 'entitlement' as the baby/child is lovingly presented to the adoptive parent/parents by the birth mother/family." (Roseman, 2000)

To me this type of ceremony is the epiphany of the perfect adoption. Most adoptions have a happy ending and as adoptive parents we all have expectations on how we foresee the adoption process. With the age of technology and changing times we must be aware that scams are becoming more prevalent with the introduction of the Internet. Each adoption is different, as is each outcome. Adoption ceremonies can be for celebrations or for the acknowledgment of our grief.

Many times when we have experienced a failed adoption we often need closure or a conclusion to the experience that will help put an end or finality on that chapter of our lives so we can move forward and start a new beginning. If this is the case, consider creating your own ceremony to fit your own individual needs to help put closure on a reclaimed or reversed adoption. Use your imagination from the candle ceremony and entrustment ceremony to create your own ceremony to recognize, acknowledge, and validate your loss. Whether you create a ceremony on a one time basis or annually it will help the healing and remind you of how special adoption is as well as help with closure on your loss.

Simply by creating your own ceremony, whether in a private ceremony, by using candles, planting a tree, flowers, or an annual event including family and friends, will lend to validation of feelings and memories that will lead to closure. Remember closure is not forgetting. You will always remember, yet the memories will be put in their appropriate place so you can move on with confidence and wisdom.

7

Other Scams or Unethical Practices

As an adoptive mom with a wonderful positive adoption experience with our first child, one of the things that would highly irritate me was seeing negative reports on adoption in the media. Now looking back I may have learned something by heeding those warnings. I do think that as our world is changing I have seen more positive media coverage and hope this only continues. Everyone has their own fantasies and expectations of adoption yet it is important to stay realistic and put the negative and positive adoption experiences into perspective.

In reality, the negative reports may have more of an impact in the public since human nature often thrives on the trials and tribulations of others. Adam Pertman reports in his book, *Adoption Nation* that, "we don't hear about most abuses because the culprits don't get caught..."(Pertman, 2000) With that statement in mind, I consider all of us lucky Sonya Furlow was convicted. Often times people are ashamed of being taken advantage of and do not know where to report such crimes. (See: Who to Contact if you Suspect Adoption Fraud, Appendix One)

Mr. Pertman also states, "that no part of the adoption world is impervious to financial seduction or subversion. And, while the number of such incidents may be low, it is steadily increasing as people realize how desperate prospective parents can get, how easily the system can be manipulated for profit, how little supervision or regulation is available, how inadequate the laws are, and how simple the internet makes it to execute scams." (Pertman, 2000)

There are many scams that take place and some are well publicized like the Twin Internet Scam. Tina Johnson, an unbonded facilitator, collected "a service fee of $6000" according to Ellen Goodman in an article in the Boston Globe entitled "Twin girls and their cyberspace fate", from a California couple and placed twin girls with them. The birth mother, Tranda Wecker, later reclaimed the babies under California state law, which allows the birth mother to change her mind in a private adoption within 90 days. Then Wecker and Johnson committed to another adoption plan and placed the children with a British couple who paid for another service fee of $12,000. Unfortunately these twin girls were shuffled between two adoptive homes, foster care, and eventually returned to their birth father. (Goodman, 2001)

Many red flags were prevalent in this scam, but went unheeded. The most basic was the large sum of money being paid for "services". According to Ellen Roseman in an article entitled "The Internet Twin Story-Who's to Blame?" she states "Tina Johnson was not bonded as a facilitator nor following California laws and statues." Ms. Johnson used the Internet to dangle the "baby carrot" in front of pre-adoptive couples. Ms. Roseman also acknowledges that, "facilitators are not alone in this. Both licensed agencies and lawyers have often been known to use questionable standards in adoption at times." (Roseman, 2000)

Ms. Roseman also notes in her article that, throughout the Twin case "no newspaper article alluded to 'counseling' being offered to the birth mother."(Roseman, 2000) Perhaps if the Allen's, the California couple, had a home study with a licensed agency or began an independent home study once the twins were in their home, Ms. Roseman notes that, "an agency adoption would have changed the revocation period from 90 days in a private adoption to 72 hours through a California agency." The Kilshaw's, the British couple, were told they could go to Arkansas to finalize the adoption. Ms. Roseman acknowledges that, "Neither Missouri nor California allowed non-resident adoptions." (Roseman, 2000) Were the Arkansas laws too lenient? There are many adoption laws in various states that need to be updated. Some are very strict others are very lax. Thus explains the importance of retaining an appropriate and competent attorney. (Roseman, 2000)

Another state that allowed non-residents with a valid home study to come into their state and adopt was Oregon, as long as the birth mother delivered in Oregon and had chosen the family. Ms. Roseman emphasized in her article that, "Oregon honors open adoption contracts which are legally binding." If another birth mother delivered her child in Oregon and had chosen the Kilshaw's, this would have given them their child legally with appropriate adoption costs and protected the birth mother. (Roseman, 2000)

It is necessary to obtain adoption attorneys or licensed agencies to navigate the maze of various laws in each state. Often the problem of locating the adoption professional is the key element. Just because an agency is licensed, a facilitator bonded, or an attorney a member of the American Academy of Adoption Attorneys does not ensure the adoption will be emotionally or financially safe or helpful. Often adoption professionals are compassionate and well meaning but their services maybe limited by being understaffed, under skilled and hindered by operating on outdated theories, thoughts and notions. (Roseman, 2000)

For example, one family in search of completing their family located an adoption attorney who appeared to have several available adoption situations. While the infant adoptions ranged between fifteen thousand and eighteen thousand dollars, the attorney also had connections with the Department of Social Services. Once the adoptive family was chosen to parent a sibling group the attorney requested a fee of seven thousand dollars to complete the adoption.

To my knowledge, adoption from social services was always known to be relatively inexpensive and usually less than two thousand dollars. What convinced the couple to pay this exorbitant fee? Once the adoption was finalized the state reimbursed the couple for all expenses incurred. Still unfortunately adoption is an industry where people rely on financial gain. While no laws were broken in this case, it certainly questions the morality of taking advantage of a system that was put in place to encourage the adoption of foster children.

Recently, some personal friends, Jack and Jane who live in the Midwest completed an adoption of a sibling group. After the adoption was finalized Jane and Jack discovered some serious health issues with their children. Was this the case of DFS not revealing the full case file? Or that fact the department was so understaffed it was not able to truly follow up on the welfare of the children. In a conversation with Jane and Jack they had revealed that they repeatedly asked the caseworker why the children were recently moved to another foster family. The caseworker responded by saying that "the little girl was throwing fits and it's the foster mom, she was just too strict." Unfortunately to this day this family is struggling with a little girl who has attachment issues, recently diagnosed with bipolar, and was emotionally and physically abused in the birth family and in the last foster home. Their lives have been turned upside down financially and emotionally trying to find services to help the child. According to Jane and Jack, their attorney saw no "red flags" nor was there any mention of this information recorded in the child's case file when they reviewed the case history. During Jane's conversations with the child's caseworker there was also no mention verbally of this information. The caseworker was relatively new to the office and shortly after the adoption she was replaced. Could this be why so many children get lost in the system? Overburdened, undereducated, burned out, under trained employees or well-meaning caseworkers anxious just to find homes for hard to place children?

Not only are pre-adoptive parents susceptible to scams and unethical treatment, prospective birth parents are at risk also. During lengthy phone interviews and emails throughout 2003, I got an up close account of one birth mother named Teresa from Idaho. Teresa had decided on an adoption plan and chose a facilitator from California by the name of Ties of Life Adoptions (not their real name), whose website boasted that they advocated open adoptions and provided counseling. Current court proceedings in this case are pending and Teresa's account of the events cut to the core. Counseling was not provided to Teresa before the birth of her twins.

In interviews with Teresa in late December 2002 and early 2003, she recounted her story that, on January 4th she gave birth to twins prematurely. She made an adoption plan even though she was warned that because she had heart problems having a child placed her in the high-risk category and could result in her death. Yet this mom decided to carry to term the pregnancy. In my opinion this was an extremely brave and unselfish decision to put her children's lives ahead of hers and her family. According to Teresa, Ties of Life Adoptions was fully aware of her medical issues and provided no help to her in obtaining medical services.

During one interview with Teresa on July 16, 2003, one of my main concerns was why she didn't receive counseling before her babies were born. Teresa said "I asked Ties of Life Adoptions about counseling, Deb, the caseworker, asked if I had a phone book, I told her never mind, I would find someone." It wasn't until after giving birth that Teresa received counseling. Teresa reported, "Deb from Ties of Life Adoptions contacted my therapist stating they would pay what wasn't covered by my insurance." In the end Teresa had to pay the counseling bill as Ties of Life never followed through as they had stated.

According to Teresa, hours after her c-section, an attorney retained on the adoptive family's behalf, by Ties of Life Adoptions was in her hospital room with termination papers. At that time the attorney referred to Ties of Life as an agency when in fact they were a facilitator. A hearing was scheduled to terminate her rights later that week. Even after Teresa informed the attorney that the doctors did not think she would be released from the hospital. The morning of the termination hearing the director of Ties of Life called her to tell her she needed to apply for Medicaid so she would not personally be held responsible for the medical bills. During this time no one explained to Teresa her rights or her right to reclaim. Teresa stated, "Ties of Life Adoptions assumed the attorney was representing both parties, but I had no representation at all until I later retained an attorney, which obviously did me little good."

Teresa reported the twins were released to the adoptive parents while she was still in the hospital. It was Teresa's understanding that the children would remain in Neonatal Intensive Care Unit for several weeks because they were premature. Yet they were released on January 12th. Teresa discovered after she was released that the adoptive parents drove 200 miles, and then caught a plane to Missouri the same day the children were released from the NICU. In defense of the adoptive parents, Maria, the director of Ties of Life Adoptions stated the adoptive parents were homesick. As reported by Teresa, the Interstate Compact papers, that allow children to be transported over state lines, were submitted on January 21st, over one week after the children had already left the state of Idaho.

When the adoptive mother left the hospital she told Teresa she would send pictures. Teresa had anticipated many pictures among other communication since this was to be an open adoption. The pictures never came. Teresa did report she received a phone call from the adoptive mom who in turn stated that when her new family had arrived at the Missouri airport they were met with balloons, gifts and banners. Teresa sadly reported, "This stung big time, as I was left with wires holding my incisions together which hurt like hell, missed three weeks of school, couldn't hold my two year old, and couldn't even comb my hair. I never saw so much as even a card from them." Within weeks after the birth of the twins, the adoptive mom closed the adoption. Even though the adoptive family has shut the door on Teresa, to this day Teresa still sends the twins small gifts and cards, hoping that the adoptive family passes them on to the children. Teresa later learned that open adoption agreements are not legally enforceable in the state of Missouri.

In an article entitled "U.S. Adoptions Get Easier", dated September 28, 2004, written by Suein Hwang, a staff reporter for the Wall Street Journal, she reports that currently "18 states have made open arrangements legally enforceable." (Hwang, 2004) When I broached this subject with Ms. Roseman, a strong advocate of open adoption records she stated that, "I have seen judges in many states honor open adoption agreements even if they are not legally enforceable. I still advise they be done and filed with the adoption paperwork."

As I continued to interview Teresa she began to raise questions when she noticed that the adoption papers stated the birth father was unknown. Teresa stated, "Repeatedly I had given the attorney and the court his full name. It wasn't until they thought I was going to reclaim the children that they finally acknowledged him."

As Teresa described the events she also reported that Mitch, the birth father, was contacted by Ties of Life and asked to deny paternity. Needless to say this case is long, complicated and unresolved. I cannot imagine the grief and anger Teresa has experienced because I have not experienced it, but I certainly have empathy.

Teresa's account of her life-altering experience reflects the same type of unethical practices that occur daily. Maybe not all of them at once and maybe on a smaller scale, but they do occur. Members of the adoption triad for whatever reason, guilt, shame, and lack of financial ability let these types of practices to continue. By choosing not to report the unethical or unlawful treatment then scam artists will continue to prey on other unsuspecting members of the triad.

According to Teresa, she had filed complaints with the Idaho, California and Missouri state Attorney Generals, the states licensing specialists, the police, the Department of Family Services, and the list goes on. What she didn't plan on was something that is seen often when a member of the triad has filed complaints against an agency, attorney, or facilitator. She was then facing threats of a gag order, of being sued, and with a restraining order. Teresa currently waits for her day in court, hoping for justice and a relationship with her children.

To put this in perspective, if you think of adoption professionals as running a business, any complaint can seriously harm their business and their livelihood. I have seen on numerous occasions where an adoption professional threatens retaliation to the point where the birth parents or adoptive parents finally succumbs for fear of financial loss and a long drawn out court battle. Yet often these threats are a diversion, just a scare tactic to end the complaints. Anyone finding him or herself in this situation should seek legal counsel and I would encourage them to not back away but to continue to fight for what is right and what they believe in.

The other scenario you often see when retaliation threats have been made is that the adoption professionals may ask the birth parents or adoptive parents to settle out of court. While this may seem like a win-win situation, it is not. With an out of court settlement the birth parents or adoptive parents will be asked to sign a document agreeing that they will not speak of their experience or the outcome in return for a monetary settlement. By doing this it leaves new or other members of the adoption triad open for the same type of unlawful or unethical practices. Unfortunately, prospective birth parents and potential adoptive parents may have to experience on their own the injustices that occur.

In discussing adoption professionals it is important to remember that this can also include adoption agencies and those employed by them. Licensed adoption agencies are sometimes considered to be a "safe" avenue in the adoption world. Just like other adoption professionals it is important to use due diligence to research and thoroughly investigate any agency you may be considering. In recent years adoption agencies have also been in the news.

One example of an agency accused of unethical practices would be the Alamo Adoption Agency (AAA) based out of San Antonio, Texas. According to Jesse Bogan in an article in the San Antonio Express-News, entitled Baby-Buying Case on Border Delayed, the Alamo Adoption Agency case "made international head-lines in September of 2002 after the arrest of Maria Dolores Bondoc." Bondoc was the Laredo, Texas representative for the agency and "was indicted on three counts of sale or purchase of a child, two counts of unlawful transport. She was also indicted on three counts of giving pregnant women a dangerous drug used to induce labor." (Bogan, 2004)

In James Kimberly's article, printed in the Houston Chronicle on September 19, 2002, entitled a Teen's Complaint Leads to Arrests at Adoption Agency, reveals that investigators allege this scam began with an advertisement placed in a "popular Mexican tabloid". "Women who responded to the ad were instructed to get to Nuevo Laredo, Mexico." Upon their arrival they were then "smuggled across the river, usually in an inner tube" by an associate of Bondoc. Once they were in Texas they stayed at Bondoc's residence until giving birth. Upon delivery of the babies the women were "convinced by whatever means necessary" to con-tinue with an adoption plan. (Kimberly, 2002)

According to Jesse Bogan, in an article entitled Baby-Buying Case on Border Delayed, printed on January 22, 2004, in the San Antonio's Express-News, the Texas "Department of Protective and Regulatory Services attempted to revoke the agency's license, but Alamo appealed" while the Laredo office was closed the agency remained open as of January 2004; "pending a decision by the State of Administrative Hearings." (Bogan, 2004) Jeorge Zarazua the author of an article entitled Mom May Sue Adoption Agency, printed on April 17, 2003 in the San Antonio Express-News Border-Bureau revealed that the owners of the Alamo Adoption Agency, "Bob and Eleanor Gray have denied involvement in or knowl-edge of illegal activities in Laredo." (Zarazua, 2003) Interestingly enough also in James Kimberly's article it reported that, "During a routine annual inspection in 1998, AAA was cited for 17 violations of the state adoption codes, including sev-eral allegations that improper payments had been made to birth mothers in Laredo." (Kimberly, 2002)

This case came to an end on May 21, 2004. According to Jesse Bogan, author of an article entitled "Baby Buyer is Heading to Prison", printed in the San Anto-nio Express-News Border Bureau, Bondoc "who pleaded no contest to charges that she illegally brought Mexican women into the United States to buy their newborn babies was sentenced…to eight years in prison. Bondoc's plea agreement also resulted in convictions of three other women who were facing similar charges. (Bogan, 2004)

The fact that Bondoc was sentenced to prison creates many questions. How long was the Alamo Adoption Agency travesty going on? How many children were illegally torn away from their mothers? Are there finalized adoptions out there that could be overturned? How many other violations existed and not made known to the public? Emotionally and morally how many other families were taken advantage of? How many other agencies are operating with these same kinds of standards? Is this a case where the Gray's had just hired someone unethical?

Ultimately, choosing an adoption professional can be one of the most important decisions a person will make. The previous examples are just a few examples of where fraud, deception and unethical practices have surfaced in the adoption world. Search the Internet; watch the news or open a newspaper and you will find a vast array of information pertaining to schemes or scams. Looking back on my experiences I wish I had not turned a blind eye to these negative news reports. Instead maybe I could have used the information to remain more objective and put a better perspective on the adoption world. Certainly the best way to choose an adoption professional is to think with your head not your heart. Realistically though, when you want to adopt so desperately or when you are contemplating making the addition of a new child into your life, thinking with you head and trusting your instincts when someone is pulling at your heartstrings will be extremely difficult.

The following list was devised to you help sort through the maze of the adoption world and to help you retain a legitimate adoption professional. These guidelines are not all inclusive and many other resources are available to help you build on these guidelines. Adoption can be a wonderful experience and there are some awesome adoption professionals. To find them you just need to educate yourself, proceed with caution and continually research in order to protect your heart and your family.

S.a.F.E. Guidelines
(Sonya Furlow Experience Guidelines)
By: Kelly Kiser-Mostrom

- Generally facilitators that "piggyback" (facilitators that network and don't necessarily screen or have their own birth mothers) are the ones that you will see advertising or "dangling" leads on the Internet. Beware of anyone "dangling" leads in front of you or an adoption professional referring to the baby as "your baby". Sometimes attorneys and agencies will do this as well. Although these situations will tug at your heartstrings it is best to find another professional. If you get a promise of a quick adoption, beware...there is no "Baby Store".

- Make sure that the adoption professional you are working with does thorough birth mother screenings. All prospective birth mothers should be offered and receive appropriate counseling. Don't be afraid to ask questions and request proof of pregnancy. A few "red flags" to watch for would be professionals who avoid answering any of your questions, someone that refuses to contact your attorney, or someone that doesn't return your phone calls promptly.

- If adoptive parents are presented with a prospective birth mother and an adoption professional is requiring money upfront, pushing for an answer in a short time period, or threatening that you will lose the match, the adoptive parents need to slow down and think with their brains and not their hearts. Why would the adoption professional be so pushy when there are many prospective adoptive parents seeking to adopt?

- Prospective adoptive parents should contact their local or state RESOLVE Chapters for referrals on adoption professionals. Once prospective adoptive parents and even prospective birth mothers have narrowed the field down to a few adoption professionals they need to investigate thoroughly, even upon doing this there may be no guarantees.

- Check for complaints with the State Attorneys General's office, the state licensing agency, local police departments, Internet sites and the Better Business Bureau (I don't put a lot of stock into the BBB. Beware if the BBB has an automated system based on the adoption professionals phone number, all the scam artist has to do is to change their phone number to get the system to eliminate negative reports). Ask lots of questions!

- Do a background check on the business and avoid businesses that have flashy marketing materials or advertise in the yellow pages. What are you looking for? Pending liens, previous court settlements and previous criminal charges. Even a well-created Internet site can be misleading. A reputable adoption professional does NOT need to seek out clients.

- You also need to check your state laws regarding adoption and the laws of the state you are adopting from. The laws in each state vary and it is often difficult to find your way through the maze. Some states do not allow facilitation services. Some states do not allow private adoptions. And some states put the baby into foster care for a time.

- Educate yourself. Read books, watch videos, attend seminars and support groups. Join various Internet egroups or check message boards on the Internet for any positive or negative reports. Network with other adoptive parents or birth parents. Keep reading!

- Pass on potential birth mothers in the early stages of pregnancy (more then 90 days from their due date) Statistically she will not follow through with the adoption plan. Whether you are dealing with a prospective birth mother or an adoption professional, question proof of pregnancy or other documents that are agreed upon, but never seem to arrive in the mail or gets lost. Especially if there seems to always be a reason or excuse for not sending you the information or if they appear to be surprised you have not received the information.

- Save copies of all correspondence, including empty envelopes with cancelled stamps, emails, receipts and any other documentation. In some adoption cases the only charges that can be brought against a scam artist is mail fraud (contact U.S. Postal Inspector) and wire transfer fraud (contact the F.B.I.)

- Beware of any adoption professional that cannot provide you with specific information that you may be requesting. With an agency, find out the state they are in and their agency license number. An adoption facilitator should be carefully looked at. In California, facilitators have to be bonded but in many states they are illegal. Request a copy of the facilitators bond or the name and address of their insurance agency where they are bonded. If you are considering an adoption attorney check with the American Academy of Adoption Attorneys (AAAA) or check with local agencies to see who they use. Contact your state Interstate Compact Office (ICPC) that is located in each states capitol. They may be helpful with procedures and knowledgeable about adoption professionals.

- If the adoption professional does not have an established business with a track record and is unknown to the adoption circle, DO NOT SEND MONEY UP-FRONT. Have your attorney review any contract before you sign one. A written contract always overrides a verbal one.

- If any adoption professional or prospective birth mother you are considering is offended by the questions you are asking they are probably not a good choice. Always make arrangements to personally meet them even if it costs a few hundred dollars. You are less likely to be scammed in an open adoption.

- Ask for a breakdown of costs. Compare their costs to others and don't be afraid to ask specifics about the contract or fees. Large fees are a big "red flag" and not necessary.

- Ask the adoption professionals what professional adoption organizations they belong too. Keep in mind though just because they belong to these organizations does not mean that someone else has checked them out. (For example a facilitator in CA has previously advertised she is "President of the Academy of CA Adoption Professionals" which many may consider a defunct group and since it currently only has 3 members.)

- The adoption scam artist often has at least one satisfied client. In order for a scam to move forward someone has to win. Don't be afraid to ask for many positive and negative references. Meeting the references in person may be helpful but more then likely it may not be feasible. Check all references and prepare a detailed list of questions for them.

- Keep a journal of detailed conversations and/or a timeline. This is a good way to pass the time while you are "waiting" and it is also helpful in determining any "red flags" or inconsistencies that may arise. Rely on your instincts.

- Be careful using the Internet. Assimilate all your information and proceed with caution. Don't rely solely on information obtained through the Net. Often people are hesitant and fearful to post negative comments about adoption professionals, for fear of retaliation.

Patience and knowledge is a key part to a S.a.F.E. adoption. I firmly believe that God has a plan for everyone. Sometimes His timeline is just different from ours. Here's wishing you a joyous and safe adoption journey!

Final Note

According to the Federal Bureau of Prisons website, www.bop.gov, Sonya Furlow was released from prison on April 11, 2003. Much earlier then her projected sentence.

Epilogue

Reflecting back to the fall of 1999, I once again remember an unseasonably warm and slightly breezy day. As Ken and I drove through a curvy road I noticed the beautiful colors of fall. A slight hint of green still remained on the trees, as the rest of the leaves were dappled with colors of red, orange and yellow.

The feelings of excitement and anxiety loomed while questions of our future was once again prevalent in the forefront of our minds. As our car came to a halt I looked out over the large peaceful lake. I noticed a few small boats, which appeared to be fishermen. To the left of us was a small playground and to the right a large area to run and play. Everything seemed so serene.

As we got out of the front of the car we turned to open the back doors. Ken's eyes met mine and he smiled, at that moment and time I knew everything in the world was right. Upon opening the back doors, out popped a charming, wise, young man of the ripe age of nine. On the other side a smiling, petite little princess that was 7 years old. Another car had pulled up behind us and parked. The caseworker exited her car carrying a shy, quiet little peanut that was one year old. They were all beautiful, bright children unsure and uncertain of their futures.

Thoughts flooded my mind. How could we be so lucky? This would be not one child but three! What was God's lesson in all of this? We never dreamed of parenting four children. As I observed them and watched in utter amazement I realized these children needed us as much as we needed them. This was the beginning of a very new and remarkable journey of completing our family.

Throughout the next several months we worked diligently on forming attachments, bonding and finalizing the adoption of our new children. Our final adoption wouldn't have been possible without the help of a working facilitator, an attorney, an agency and the Department of Family Services. It took the services of all these professionals to make our dreams come true. Through all the turmoil and lessons we learned, I firmly believe there is a time and place for everything. We may not always know the reasons but in the end we were blessed. Education, knowledge, patience and faith were the keys to our successful adoption journey. I am happy to say we are now proud parents of four children! Many blessing to you all!

APPENDIX A

Who to Contact if you Suspect Adoption Fraud

Initially, once you have discovered you're the victim of adoption fraud many emotions will surface. It may be hard to concentrate or think clearly. Reporting the crime or suspected fraud may be emotionally difficult. By telling your story you will be able to start the healing process and save someone else from the emotional turmoil of *The Cruelest Con*. The following steps outline whom to contact should you be exposed to such a crime. I urge anyone who suspects adoption fraud to file the necessary complaints if not for you, to protect other unsuspecting victims. Make all complaints consistent, stick to the facts, be specific, and be detailed. Finally, keep a record or file of complaints and acknowledgements for future reference.

Contact

1. **Your Local Police Department**

2. **The FBI**

3. **The U.S. Postal Inspector**

4. **The State Licensing Specialist, local adoption agencies, facilitators, adoption attorneys**

5. **Your State Attorney General's Office**

6. **The National Fraud Information Center (www.fraud.com)**

7. **Post factual complaints on the Internet message boards**

8. **Post factual complaints with newsgroups (adoptionscams@yahoo.com)**

9. Write letters to your State Representatives, State Senators and Governor

10. Contact the media, print, radio and television.

Copy all your information…. only hand over originals if you have copies of everything.

APPENDIX B

Internet Resources

Internet Sites:

www.adopting.com
www.adopting.org
www.Adoption.com
www.fertilethoughts.com
www.adoptionattorneys.com
www.adopthelp.com
www.adoptionnetwork.com
www.adoptivefamilies.com
www.adoptioninsight.org

Internet Sites for Adoption Books/Magazine Resources

www.coopadopt.com
www.pactadopt.com
www.tapestrybooks.com
www.r2press.com
www.adopt-usa.com/rootsandwings
www.perspectivepress.com
www.adoptioninsight.org

Other Adoption Internet Sites

www.adoptionprofessionals.com
www.openadoption.com
www.fosterparenting.com
www.adoptionsites.com

Sites to File Complaints

www.ifccfbi.gov
www.fraud.com
www.bbb.org
www.consumer.gov/sentinel/index.html

APPENDIX C

Recommended Reading

Adoption Issues

Freundlich, M., & Peterson, L. (1998). *Wrongful Adoption-Law and Policy.* Washington, DC: Child Welfare League of America.

Hollinger, J. (2004). *Families by Law: An Adoption Reader* N. R. Cahn, & J. Hollinger (Eds.). New York, NY: New York University Press.

Maguire Pavao, J. (1999). *The Family of Adoption.* Boston, MA: Beacon Press.

Pertman, A. (2001). *Adoption Nation: How the Adoption Revolution is Transforming America.* New York, NY: Basic Books.

Grief and Loss

Childs-Gowell, E. (1992). *Good Grief Rituals: Tools for Healing: A Healing Companion.* Barrytown, NY: Station Hill Press.

James, J. W., & Friedman, R. (1998). *The Grief Recovery Handbook: The Action Program for Moving Beyond Death, Divorce, and Other Losses* (Rev. ed.). New York, NY: HarperCollins.

Jewett Jarratt, C. (1994). *Helping Children Cope with Separation and Loss* (Rev. ed.). Boston, MA: Harvard Common PR.

Roles, P. (1989). *Saying Goodbye to a Baby: Birth parents Guide to Loss and Grief in Adoption (Saying Goodbye to a Baby Vol. 1).* Washington, DC: Child Welfare League of America.

Roles, P. (1990). *Saying Goodbye to a Baby: A Counselor's Guide to Birth parent Loss and Grief in Adoption (Saying Goodbye to a Baby Vol.2)*. Washington, DC: Child Welfare League of America.

Romanchik, B. (1999). *Birth parent Grief*. Royal Oak, MI: R-Squared Press.

Westberg, G. E. (1979). *Good Grief: A Constructive Approach to the Problem of Loss*. Minneapolis, MN: Augsburg Fortress Press.

Open Adoption

Gritter, J. (1997). *The Spirit of Open Adoption*. Washington, DC: Child Welfare League of America.

Kaplan Roszia, S., & Ruskai Melina, L. (1993). *The Open Adoption Experience: A Complete Guide for Adoptive and Birth Families-From making the Decision Through the Child's Growing Years* (1st ed.). New York, NY: HarperCollins Publishers, Inc.

Martinez-Dorner, P. M. (1998). *How to Open an Adoption: A guide for parents and birth parents of minors*. Royal Oak, MI: Insight.

Rappaport, B. M. (1997). *The Open Adoption Book: A Guide to Adoption without Tears* (Rev. ed.). New York, NY: John Wiley and Sons.

Silber, K., & Martinez Dorner, P. (1990). *Children of Open Adoption and Their Families*. San Antonio, TX: Corona Publishing Co.

Silber, K., & Speedlin, P. (1998). *Dear Birth mother: Thank you for our baby* (3rd ed.). San Antonio, TX: Corona Publishing Co.

Triad, Search and Reunion Stories

Back McKay, L. (1998). *Shadow Mother: Stories of Adoption and Reunion*. St. Cloud, MN: North Star Press of St. Cloud.

Franklin, L. C. (1998). *May the Circle be Unbroken: An Intimate Journey into the Heart of Adoption* (1st ed.). New York, NY: Harmony Books.

Howard, S. (2003). *Finding Me In a Paper Bag: Searching For Both Sides Now*. Baltimore, MD: Gateway Press, Inc.

McColm, M. (1993). *Adoption reunions: A Book for Adoptees, Birth Parents and Adoptive Families.* Toronto, ON Canada: Second Story Press.

Russell, M. (1996). *Adoption Wisdom: A Guide to the Issues and Feelings of Adoption.* Santa Monica, CA: Broken Branch Productions.

Schaefer, C. (1992). *The Other Mother: A Woman's Love for the Child she gave up for Adoption.* New York, NY: Soho Press, Inc.

Wadia-Ells, S. (1992). *The Adoption Reader: Birth Mothers, Adoptive Mothers and Adoptive Daughters Tell Their Stories.* Seattle, WA: Seal Press.

Birth parents

Bloch Jones, M. (2000). *Birth mothers: Women Who Have Relinquished Babies for Adoption Tell Their Stories.* New York, NY: The Authors Guild; Backinprint.com.

Foge, L., & Mosconi, G. (2004). *The Third Choice: A Woman's Guide to Placing a Child for Adoption.* Oakland, CA: Third Choice Books.

Gritter, J. L. (1999). *Lifegivers: Framing the Birth parent Experience in Open Adoption.* Washington, DC: Child Welfare League of America.

Guttman, J. (1999). *The Gift Wrapped in Sorrow: A Mother's Quest for Healing (1st ed.).* JMJ Publishing.

Martin Mason, M. (1995). *Out of the Shadows: Birth fathers' Stories.* Edina, MN: O.J. Howard Publishing.

Romanchik, B. (1995). *A Birth mother's Book of Memories.* Royal Oak, MI: R-Squared Press.

Severson, R. W. (1991). *Dear Birth father.* Dallas, TX: House of Tomorrow Productions.

Wolch-Marsh, M. J. (1996). *A Birth Mother's Day Planner* (1st ed.). Royal Oak, MI: R-Squared Press.

International Adoption

Ebejer Petertyl, M. (2002). *International Adoption Travel Journal* (Rev. ed.). Grand Rapids, MI: Folio One Pub.

Maclean, J. (2004). *The Russian Adoption Handbook: How to Adopt from Russia, Ukraine, Kazakhstan, Bulgaria, Belarus, Georgia, Azerbaijan and Moldova.* Lincoln, NE: iUniverse Star.

Nelson-Erichsen, J., & Erichsen, H. R. (2003). *How to Adopt Internationally: A Guide for Agency-Directed and Independent Adoptions, Revised and Updated* (Rev. ed.). Fort Worth, TX: Mesa House Publishing.

Woodard, S. L. (2002). *Daughter from Afar: A Family's International Adoption Story.* Lincoln, NE: iUniverse, Inc.

Parenting and Social Situations

Gray, D. D. (2002). *Attaching in Adoption: Practical Tools for Today's Parents.* Indianapolis, IN: Perspectives Press.

Steinberg, G., & Hall, B. (2000). *Inside Transracial Adoption.* Indianapolis, IN: Perspective Press.

Adoptees

Eldridge, S. (1999). *Twenty Things Adopted Kids Wish their Adoptive Parents Knew.* New York, NY: Dell Publishing.

Newton Verrier, N. (2003). *Coming Home to Self: The Adopted Child Grows Up.* Lafayette, CA: Verrier Publications.

Newton Verrier, N. (1997). *The Primal Wound: Understanding the Adopted Child.* Lafayette, CA: Verrier Publications.

Rituals

Lieberman, C., & Bufferd, R. (1998). *Creating Ceremonies: Innovative Ways to Meet Adoption Challenges.* Ithaca, NY: Zieg, Tucker & Theisen, Inc.

Martin Mason, M., & Parks, D. (1995). *Designing Rituals of Adoption: For the Religious and Secular Community.* Minneapolis, MN: Resources for Adoptive Parents.

APPENDIX D

Other Resources

Information

National Adoption Information Clearinghouse
P.O. Box 1182
Washington, DC 20013
(888) 251-0075
www.calib.com.naic

Evan B. Donaldson Adoption Institute (For Adoption Ethics)
Adam Pertman, Executive Director
525 Broadway
New York, NY 10012
(212) 925-4089
Fax (775) 796-6592
www.adoptioninstitute.org

The Adoption Education Institute
New Hope Communications
2472 Broadway, Ste. 377
New York, NY 10025
Phone (646) 366-0833
www.adoptioneducation.org

American Academy of Adoption Attorneys
P.O. Box 33053
Washington, DC 20033-0053
(202) 832-2222
www.adoptionattorneys.org

The Adoption Exchange
14232 E. Evans Avenue
Aurora, CO 80014
(800) 451-5246
Fax: (303) 755-1339
www.adoptex.org

The Center for Adoption Support and Education Inc.
11120 New Hampshire Avenue, Ste. 205
Silver Springs, MD 20904
(301) 593-9200
Fax: (301) 593-9203
www.adoptionsupport.org

The Joint Council of International Children's Services
1320 Nineteenth St. NW, Suite 200
Washington. DC 20036
(202) 429-0400
www.jcics.org

National Resource Center for Special Needs Adoption
16250 Northland Drive, Suite 120
Southfield, MI 48075
(248) 443-7080
Fax: (248) 443-7099
www.spaulding.org

Better Business Bureau
Council of Better Business Bureau
4200 Wilson Boulevard, Suite 800
Arlington, VA 22203-1838
(703) 276-0100
Fax: (703) 525-8277
www.bbb.org

Council on Accreditation for Children and Families Services, Inc.
120 Wall Street, 11th Floor
New York, NY 10005

(212) 797-3000/(800) COA-8088
Fax: (212) 797-1428
www.coanet.org

Adoption Support

Cooperative Adoption Consulting
54 Wellington Avenue
San Anselmo, CA 94960
(415) 453-0902
Fax: (415) 455-9449
www.coopadopt.org

Council on Adoptable Children
666 Broadway, Suite 820
New York, NY 10012
(212) 475-02222
Fax: (212) 475-1972
www.coac.org

National Adoption Center/Faces of Adoption
1500 Walnut Street, Suite 701
Philadelphia PA 19102
(215) 735-9988/(800) 862-3678
www.adopt.org

North American Council on Adoptable Children
970 Raymond Avenue, Suite 106
St. Paul, MN 55114
(651) 644-3036
www.nacac.org

PACT, An Adoption Alliance
4179 Piedmont Avenue, Suite 330
Oakland, CA 94611
(510) 243-9460
Fax (510) 243-9970

(800) 750-7590 (Birth parent Line)
(888) 448-8277 (Adoptive Parent Peer Support Line)
www.pactadopt.org

Adoption Network Cleveland
Betsie Norris-Executive Director
1667 East 40th Street
Cleveland, Ohio 44103
(216) 881-7511
Fax (216) 881-7510
www.adoptionnetwork.org

Child Welfare League of America
440 First Street, N.W.
Washington, DC 20001
(202) 638-2952
www.cwla.org

Dave Thomas Foundation for Adoption
4288 West Dublin—Granville Road
Dublin, OH 43017
(614) 764-3100
www.nac.adopt.org/wendy.html

Council for Equal Rights in Adoption
Attention: Joe Soll
356 E. 74th Street, Suite 2
New York, NY 10021
(212) 988-0110
www.adoptioncrossroads.org

Association for Treatment and Training in the Attachment of Children
(ATTACh)
P.O. Bow 11347
Columbia, SC 29211
(866) 453-8224
www.attach.org

Adoption Membership/Advocacy/Search

American Adoption Congress
1025 Connecticut Avenue
N.W. Washington, DC 20036
(202) 483-3399
www.americanadoptioncongress.org

Bastard Nation (adoptees)
21904 Marine View Drive
Des Moines, WA 98198
(415) 704-3166
www.bastards.org

Adoptees Liberty Movement Association
P.O. Box 727 Radio City Station
New York, NY 10101
(212) 581-1568
www.almanet.com

Concerned United Birth parents, Inc.
P.O. Box 230457
Encinitas, CA 92023
(800) 822-2777
Fax (760) 929-1879
www.cubirthparents.org

National Council for Single Adoptive Parents
P.O. Box 15084
Chevy Chase, MD 20825
(202) 966-6367
www.adopting.org/ncsapfrm.html

Family Pride Coalition (Gay/Lesbian)
P.O. Box 34337
San Diego, CA 92163
(619) 296-0199
www.glpci.org

RESOLVE (Infertility/Adoption)
1310 Broadway
Somerville, MA 02144
(617) 623-0744
www.resolve.org

International Soundex Reunion Registry
P.O. Box 2131
Carson City, NV 89702
(775) 882-7755
www.plumsite.com/isrr/index.html

Post Adoption Center For Education & Research (PACER)
P.O. Box 31146
Oakland, CA 94604
(888) 746-0514
www.pacer-adoption.org

APPENDIX E

Glossary

Terms are interpreted slightly differently throughout the Child Abuse and Neglect, Child Welfare, and Adoption fields. Commonly held definitions for terms are identified in this Glossary.

Abandonment

Desertion of a child by a parent or adult primary care giver with no provisions for continued childcare nor with any apparent intention to return to resume care giving.

Abuse and Neglect

Physical, sexual and/or emotional maltreatment. Child abuse and neglect is defined as any recent act or failure to act resulting in imminent risk of serious harm, death, serious physical or emotional harm, sexual abuse, or exploitation of a child (a person under the age of 18, unless the child protection law of the State in which the child resides specifies a younger age for cases not involving sexual abuse) by a parent or caretaker (including any employee of a residential facility or any staff person providing out-of-home care) who is responsible for the child's welfare. Abuse and neglect are defined in both Federal and State legislation. The Federal CAPTA legislation provides a foundation for States by identifying a minimum set of acts or behaviors that characterize maltreatment. This legislation also defines what acts are considered physical abuse, neglect, and sexual abuse (**maltreatment**).

Access veto systems

Type of reunion registry system. The veto is a document filed by one party to the adoption which registers that person's refusal to be contacted or denial of release of identifying information. In an access veto or nondisclosure request system, an adopted adult may receive identifying information about another party if no veto is on file. Some States may have provisions for a contact veto, permitting a party seeking information access to identifying information, including an original birth certificate, but prohibiting contact between the parties.

Active registries

Reunion registries, which do not require that both parties register their consent. Once one party is registered, a designated individual (often an agency or court representative) is assigned to contact those persons being sought and determine their wishes for the release of information.

Adoptee

An adopted person. Some adopted persons object to being called an "adoptee" because: (1) It distinguishes an adopted child from a birth child in the same family. (One does not say, "This is my birth son, Johnny.") (2) It implies adoption is the central fact of that person's life (which, of course, it may be).

Adoption

A court action in which an adult assumes legal and other responsibilities for another, usually a minor.

Adoption agency

An organization, usually licensed by the State, that provides services to birth parents, adoptive parents, and children who need families. Agencies may be public or private, secular or religious, for profit or nonprofit.

Adoption assistance

Monthly or one-time only subsidy payments to help adoptive parents raise children with special needs. These payments were initially made possible by the enactment of the Adoption Assistance and Child Welfare Act of 1980 (P.L. 96-272), which provided Federal funding for children eligible under title IV-E of the Social Security Act; States also fund monthly payments for children with special needs who are not eligible for federally funded subsidy payments. "Adoption assistance" can also refer to any help given to adoptive parents.

Adoption attorney

A legal professional who has experience with filing, processing, and finalizing adoptions in a court having jurisdiction.

Adoption benefits

Compensation to workers through employer-sponsored programs. Some examples of such benefits are financial assistance or monetary reimbursement for the expenses of adopting a child, or provision of "parental" or "family" leave.

Adoption consultant

Anyone who helps with the placement of a child, but specifically someone who makes it his or her private business to facilitate adoptions.

Adoption disruption

The interruption of an adoption prior to finalization—sometimes called a "failed adoption" or a "failed placement".

Adoption dissolution

The interruption or "failure" of an adoption after finalization that requires court action.

Adoption exchange

An organization which recruits adoptive families for children with special needs using print, radio, television and Internet recruitment, as well as matching parties (which bring together prospective adoptive parents, waiting children and their social workers in a child-focused setting). Adoption exchanges can be local, state, regional, national or international in scope.

Adoption facilitator

Individual whose business involves connecting birth parents and prospective adoptive parents for a fee (only allowed in a few States).

Adoption insurance (adoption cancellation insurance)

Insurance which protects against financial loss which can be incurred after a birth mother changes her mind and decides not to place her child for adoption.

Adoption petition

The legal document through which prospective parents request the court's permission to adopt a specific child.

Adoption placement

The point at which a child begins to live with prospective adoptive parents; the period before the adoption is finalized.

Adoption plan

Birth parents' decisions to allow their child to be placed for adoption.

Adoption reversal

Reclaiming of a child (originally voluntarily placed with adoptive parents) by birth parent(s) who have had a subsequent change of heart. State laws vary in defining time limits and circumstances under which a child may be reclaimed.

Adoption subsidies

Federal or State adoption benefits (also known as **adoption assistance**) designed to help offset the short- and long-term costs associated with adopting children who need special services. To be eligible for the Federal IV-E subsidy program, children must meet each of the following characteristics:

- a court has ordered that the child cannot or should not be returned to the birth family
- the child has special needs, as determined by the state's definition of special needs
- a "reasonable effort" has been made to place the child without a subsidy
- the child must have been eligible for Supplemental Security Income (SSI) at the time of the adoption, or the child's birth family must have been receiving- or eligible to receive-Aid for Families with Dependent Children (AFDC).

Benefits available through subsidy programs vary by State, but commonly include:

- **monthly cash payments**—up to an amount that is $1 less than the foster care payment the state would have made if the child were still in basic family foster care
- **medical assistance**—through the federal program (and some state programs), Medicaid benefits

- **social services**—post-adoption services such as respite care, counseling, day care, etc.

- **nonrecurring adoption expenses**—a one-time reimbursement (depending upon the state, between $400 and $2,000) for costs such as adoption fees, court costs, attorney fees, physical and psychological examinations, and other expenses related to the legal adoption of a child with special needs.

Before adopting a child with special needs, ask your agency about the availability of federal and state subsidies.

Adoption tax credits

Non-refundable credit which reduces taxes owed by adoptive parents who claim adoption expense reimbursement under P.L. 104-188; may be claimed on Federal taxes (and in some States with similar legislation, on State taxes).

Adoption tax exclusions

IRS provisions in the Federal tax code which allow adoptive parents to exclude cash or other adoption benefits for qualifying adoption expenses received from a private-sector employer when computing the family's adjusted gross income for tax purposes.

Adoption triad

The three major parties in an adoption: birth parents, adoptive parents, and adopted child. Also called "adoption triangle" or "adoption circle."

Adult adoption

The adoption of a person over the age of majority (as defined in State law).

Agency adoption

Adoptive placements made by licensed organizations that screen prospective adoptive parents and supervise the placement of children in adoptive homes until the adoption is finalized.

Alcohol-related birth defects

Physical or cognitive deficits in a child which result from maternal alcohol consumption during pregnancy—includes but is not limited to **Fetal Alcohol Syndrome (FAS)** and **Fetal Alcohol Effect (FAE)**.

Anti-social behavior

Actions deviating sharply from the social norm. Children with such behaviors commonly skip school, get into fights, run away from home, persistently lie, use drugs or alcohol, steal, vandalize property, and violate school and home rules.

Apostille

A simplified certification of public (including notarized) documents used in countries that participate in a Hague Convention. This simplified form contains numbered fields (which allow the data to be understood by all participating countries regardless of the official language of the issuing country). The completed apostille form certifies the authenticity of the document's signature, the capacity in which the person signing the document has acted, and identifies the seal/stamp, which the document bears. Documents needed for intercountry adoptions require the attachment of an apostille (rather than authentication forms) if the foreign country participates in the convention.

Artificial insemination

Impregnation of a woman by one of many possible artificial reproductive technologies (ARTs).

Attachment

The ability of a child to form significant and stable emotional connections with other people, beginning in early infancy with one or more primary caretakers. Failure to establish such connections before the age of five may result in difficulties with social relationships as severe as **reactive attachment disorder.**

Attention deficit disorder (ADD)

A lifelong developmental disability (with onset in infancy, childhood or adolescence) that affects a child's ability to concentrate and control impulses. A child who has ADD is not hyperactive, but often has problems sustaining attention in task or play activities, difficulty in persisting with tasks to completion, and concentrating for longer periods of time.

Attention deficit hyperactivity disorder (ADHD)

A lifelong developmental disability (with onset in infancy, childhood or adolescence) that involves problems with attention span, impulse control, and activity level at home, at school or at work. Typical behaviors include: fidgeting with hands or squirming in seat; difficulty remaining seated when required; distractibility; difficulty waiting for turns in groups; difficulty staying on task with chores or play activities; difficulty playing quietly; excessive talking; inattention; restlessness; and engaging in physically dangerous activities without considering consequences.

Autistic disorder

A pervasive developmental disturbance with onset before age three, characterized by markedly abnormal or impaired development in social interaction and communication and a markedly restricted array of activity and interests. Manifestations of the disorder vary greatly depending on the developmental level and age of the individual. Autistic children can be withdrawn and show little interest in others or in typical childhood activities and instead exhibit repetitive and stereotyped patterns of behavior, interests and activities.

Bipolar disorder

A category of mental illnesses in which mood and affect are disturbed—characterized by irregular cycles of mania and/or depression. During manic periods, the individual may be in a very elevated mood and exhibit symptoms of hyperactivity, wakefulness, and distractibility or irritability. In very severe episodes, psychotic symptoms may also be present. Individuals experiencing depressive periods can exhibit sustained symptoms of depressed mood, diminished pleasure or interest in most activities, fatigue, sleep disturbance (either insomnia or hypersomnia), weight loss or weight gain, and slowed thinking.

Birth parent

A child's biological parent.

Black market adoption

An adoption in which one or more parties make a profit from a child placement, as opposed to receiving payment for providing counseling, location, or other services.

Boarder babies

Infants abandoned in hospitals because of the parents' inability to care for them. These babies are usually born HIV-positive or drug addicted.

Bonding

The process of developing lasting emotional ties with one's immediate caregivers; seen as the first and primary developmental task of a human being and central to the person's ability to relate to others throughout life.

Central auditory processing disorder

A condition in which an individual has difficulty comprehending and integrating information that is heard, although hearing is normal. Central auditory processing disorder occurs when the ear and the brain do not coordinate fully. The causes of this disorder are varied and can include head trauma, lead poisoning, possibly chronic ear infections and other unknown reasons. Because there are many different possibilities or even combinations of causes each child must be individually assessed.

Cerebral palsy

A non-hereditary condition, which results from brain damage before, during, or after birth. Children with cerebral palsy lack muscle control in one or more parts of their bodies or may experience speech and language difficulties, depending on the area of the brain damaged. Individuals with cerebral palsy can possess very normal mental functions.

Certification

The approval process (detailed in State laws or regulations) that takes place to ensure, insofar as possible, that adoptive or foster parents are suitable, dependable, and responsible. "Certification" of documents involves a seal or apostille required by law or regulation affixed to a public document (such as a birth or marriage certificate or court record) to attest to its authenticity or to a general document to attest that the document. has been notarized by an authorized official.

Closed adoption

An adoption that involves total confidentiality and sealed records.

Concurrent planning

A process used in foster care case management by which child welfare staff work toward family reunification and, at the same time, develop an alternative permanency plan for the child (such as permanent placement with a relative, or adoption) should family reunification efforts fail. Concurrent planning is intended to reduce the time a child spends in foster care before a child is placed with a permanent family.

Conduct disorder

A condition characterized by a repetitive and persistent pattern of behavior which violates the basic rights of others or major age-appropriate societal norms or rules. A child or teen with conduct disorder may:

- display aggressive conduct (bully or threaten others; initiate fights; use weapons that could cause serious harm; force someone into sexual activity; be physically aggressive or cruel to people or animals);

- engage in nonaggressive behaviors that result in property loss or damage;

- engage in deceitfulness or theft (steal; or lie or break promises to obtain goods or to avoid debts or obligations)

- persistently engage in serious violations of rules that lead to confrontations with parents, school suspensions or expulsion, problems in the workplace, or legal difficulties (staying out after dark without permission; running away from home; truancy; etc.).

Conduct disorder may lead to the development of Antisocial Personality Disorder during adulthood.

Confidential Intermediary

State employee or trained volunteer sanctioned by the courts, who is given access to sealed adoption files for the purpose of conducting a search. A confidential intermediary may be hired by the inquiring party to conduct searches for an adopted adult or birth parent or other birth relatives (depending on State laws), make contact with each party, and obtain each person's consent or denial for the release of information. Depending on the particular laws of the State, contact may be attempted once, after a specific time period, or the file may be closed permanently if the party being sought cannot be found.

Confidentiality

The legally required process of keeping identifying or other significant information secret; the principle of ethical practice which requires social workers and other professional not to disclose information about a client without the client's consent.

Consent to adopt or consent to adoption

Legal permission for the adoption to proceed.

Co-parenting

A long-term (formal or informal) agreement to support the needs of children with developmental disabilities by which extra caregivers support parents by providing ongoing respite parenting when needed.

Custody

The care, control, and maintenance of a child, which can be legally awarded by the court to an agency (in abuse and neglect cases) or to parents (in divorce, separation, or adoption proceedings). Child welfare departments retain legal custody and control of major decisions for a child in foster care; foster parents do not have legal custody of the children they care for.

De facto A term meaning "in actual fact", "in deed" or "actually", regardless of legal or normative standards. In a legal context, the phrase refers to an action or a state of affairs which must be accepted for all practical purposes, but which has no legal basis. A "de facto family" is a "psychological family" in which members have ties to each other even though they are relatives by birth or marriage and do not have a legal document recognizing their relationship.

De facto adoption

A legal agreement to adopt a child according to the laws of a particular State which will result in a legal adoption process once the adoption petition is filed with the appropriate court; an **equitable adoption**.

Decree of adoption

A legal order that finalizes an adoption.

Dependent child

A child who is in the custody of the county or State child welfare system.

Developmental disability

A severe, chronic impairment (with onset before age 22 and which is likely to continue indefinitely) which creates substantial functional limitations in three or more of the following areas of major life activity: self care, language, learning, mobility, self-direction, potential for independent living and potential for economic self-sufficiency as an adult. The condition can be attributed to one or more mental or physical impairments, which require specific and lifelong or extended care that is individually planned and coordinated.

Disclosure

The release or transmittal of previously hidden or unknown information.

Disruption

The term **disruption** is used to describe an adoption that ends before it is legally finalized, resulting in the child's legal custody reverting back to the agency or court that made the original placement and the child returning to foster care and/ or to other adoptive parent(s).

Dissolution

The term **dissolution** is used to describe an adoption that fails after finalization, resulting in the child's legal custody reverting back to the agency or court that made the original placement and the child returning to foster care and/or to other adoptive parent(s).

Dossier

A set of legal documents, which are used in an international adoption to process a child's adoption or assignment of guardianship in the foreign court.

Down syndrome

A genetic disorder (caused by the presence of an extra chromosome), which results in physical and mental abnormalities. Physical characteristics include a flattened face, widely spaced and slanted eyes, smaller head size and lax joints. Mental retardation is also typical, though there are wide variations in mental ability, behavior, and developmental progress. Possible related health problems include poor resistance to infection, hearing loss, gastrointestinal problems, and heart defects.

Emotional disturbance

Severe, pervasive or chronic emotional/affective condition, which prevents a child from performing everyday tasks. This condition is characterized by an inability to build or maintain relationships, inappropriate behaviors or feelings under normal circumstances, a pervasive mood of unhappiness or depression, or a tendency to develop physical symptoms or fears related to personal or school problems. Children may require special classrooms and teachers trained to help children with these special needs. School systems may have varying "levels" and processes for educational planning.

Equitable adoption

The legal process used in some States to establish inheritance rights of a child, when the prospective adoptive parent had entered into an oral contract to adopt the child and the child was placed with the parent but the adoption was not finalized before the parent died.

Employer Assistance

Adoption benefits provided to employees by employers which may include direct cash assistance for adoption expenses, reimbursement of approved adoption expenses, paid or unpaid leave (beyond federal leave requirements established through the Family and Medical Leave Act of 1993), and resource and referral services. For a list of employers who provide benefits, call the National Adoption Center at (800)-TO-ADOPT.

Extended family

A child's relatives (other than parents) such as aunts, uncles, grandparents, and sometimes even close friends.

Family preservation

A program of supportive social services designed to keep families together by providing services to children and families in their home. It is based on the premise that birth families are the preferred means of providing family life for children.

Fetal alcohol effect (FAE)

A disorder associated with cognitive and behavioral difficulties in children whose birth mothers drank alcohol while pregnant. Symptoms are similar to fetal alcohol syndrome (FAS) but less severe or comprehensive.

Fetal alcohol syndrome (FAS)

Birth defects, and serious life-long mental and emotional impairments that may result from heavy maternal alcohol consumption during pregnancy. Symptoms of mental and emotional deficits may include significant learning and behavioral disorders (including attention deficits and hyperactivity), diminished cause-and-effect thinking, poor social judgment, and impulsive behaviors.

Fictive kin

People not related by birth or marriage that have an emotionally significant relationship with an individual.

Finalization

The final legal step in the adoption process; involves a court hearing during which the judge orders that the adoptive parents become the child's legal parents.

Foster-adoption

A child placement in which birth parents' rights have not yet been severed by the court or in which birth parents are appealing the court's decision but foster parents agree to adopt the child if/when parental rights are terminated. Social workers place the child with specially trained foster-adopt parents who will work with the child during family reunification efforts but who will adopt the child if the child becomes available for adoption. The main reason for making such a placement, also called legal-risk adoption, is to spare the child another move.

Foster children

Children who have been placed in the State's or county's legal custody because their birth parents were deemed abusive, neglectful, or otherwise unable to care for them.

Foster parents

State- or county-licensed adults who provide a temporary home for children whose birth parents are unable to care for them.

Genealogy

A family's genetic "line", family tree, or a record of such ancestry.

Grief

A feeling of emotional deprivation or loss. Grief may be experienced by each member of the adoption triad at some point.

Group home

A homelike setting in which a number of unrelated children live for varying time periods. Group homes may have one set of house parents or may have a rotating staff and some therapeutic or treatment group homes have specially-trained staff to assist children with emotional and behavioral difficulties.

Guardian

Person who fulfills some of the responsibilities of the legal parent role, although the courts or birth parents may continue to hold some jurisdiction of the child. Guardians do not have the same reciprocal rights of inheritance as birth or adoptive parents. Guardianship is subject to ongoing supervision by the court and ends at the child's majority or by order of the court.

Guardian ad litem (GAL)

A person, often an attorney, appointed by the court to represent the interests of a child, a ward, or an unborn infant in a particular court case. The status of guardian ad litem exists only within the confines of the particular court case in which the appointment occurs.

Home study

A process through which prospective adoptive parents are educated about adoption and evaluated to determine their suitability to adopt.

I-600 and I-600A visa petition

An official request to the US Immigration and Naturalization Service (INS) to classify an orphan as an immediate relative—providing expedited processing and issuance of a visa to allow the child to enter the United States after having been adopted abroad or in order to be adopted in the United States.

Identifying information

Information on birth parents that discloses their identities.

Independent adoption

An adoption facilitated by those other than caseworkers associated with an agency. Facilitators may be attorneys, physicians, or other intermediaries. In some States independent adoptions are illegal.

Independent living

A type of placement that provides life-skills training to youth to assist them to acquire the skills they will need to live independently as adults. The program is designed for children who are "aging out" of foster care and for whom there is no other permanency plan.

Indian Child Welfare Act (ICWA)

A federal law (Public Law 95-608) regarding the placement of Native-American children which establishes the tribe's sovereignty as a separate nation over the welfare of children who are tribal members of who are eligible for tribal membership.

Infertility

The inability to bear children.

IEP

Abbreviation for Individualized Educational Plan, a plan for educational support services and outcomes developed for students enrolled in special education programs.

IEP

Acronym for Interethnic Placement provisions; refers to Section 1808 of P.L. 104-188, Removal of Barriers to Interethnic Adoption, which affirms the prohibition contained in the Multi-Ethnic Placement Act of 1994 against delaying or denying the placement of a child for adoption or foster care on the basis of race, color or national origin of the foster or adoptive parents or of the child involved [42 USC 1996b].

INS

INS has changed its name to the U.S. Citizenship and Immigration Services, now a bureau under the U.S. Department of Homeland Security.

Institutionalization

The placement of children in hospitals, institutions, or orphanages. Placement in institutions during early critical developmental periods and for lengthy periods is often associated with developmental delays due to environmental deprivation, poor staff-child ratios, or lack of early stimulation.

Intercountry or international adoption

The adoption of a child who is a citizen of one country by adoptive parents who are citizens of a different country.

Interstate compact

A voluntary agreement between two or more States designed to address common problems of the States concerned.

Interstate Compact on Adoption and Medical Assistance (ICAMA)

An agreement between member states that governs the interstate delivery of and payment for medical services and adoption assistance payments/subsidies for adopted children with special needs. The agreements are established by the laws of the States, which are parties to the Compact.

Interstate Compact on the Placement of Children (ICPC)

An agreement regulating the placement of children across state lines. All 50 states, the District of Columbia, and the U.S. Virgin Islands have independently adopted the ICPC as statutory law in their respective jurisdictions.

Kinship care

The full-time nurturing of a child by someone related to the child by family ties or by prior relationship connection (**fictive kin**).

Learning disabilities (LD)

One or more impairments in reading, mathematics and/or written expression skills which interfere with academic performance in school or in activities of daily living requiring those skills. Performance on standardized tests below that expected for age, schooling and level of intelligence are used as preliminary diagnostic tools to identify areas where children are experiencing problems. Children with learning disabilities may be of average or above average intelligence, but have difficulty learning, sorting, and storing information. Some children find learning in a regular classroom difficult and LD classes may be recommended to help them achieve their potential in school.

Legal custody

Restraint of or responsibility for a person according to law, such as a guardian's authority (conferred by the court) over the person or property (or both) of his ward.

Legal guardian

A person who has legal responsibility for the care and management of a person who is incapable of administering his own affairs. In the case of a minor child, the guardian is charged with the legal responsibility for the care and management of the child and of the minor child's estate.

Legal risk placement

Placement of a child in a prospective adoptive family when a child is not yet legally free for adoption. Before a child can be legally adopted by another family, parental rights of his or her birth parents must be terminated. In a "legal risk" adoptive placement either this termination of parental rights has not yet occurred, or it is being contested. In some cases, termination of parental rights is delayed until a specific adoptive family has been identified.

Legally free

A child whose birth parents' rights have been legally terminated so that the child is "free" to be adopted by another family.

Life book

A pictorial and written representation of the child's life designed to help the child make sense of his unique background and history. The life book includes birth parents, other relatives, birthplace and date, etc and can be put together by social workers, foster and/or adoptive parents working with the child.

Long-term foster care

The intentional and planned placement of a child in foster care for an extended period of time. After the goal of adoption has been explored and not selected, and relative options are not feasible, a goal of planned long-term foster care may be seen as a viable goal. Increasingly some States child welfare systems no longer view long-term foster care as a placement alternative.

Loss

A feeling of emotional deprivation that is experienced at some point in time. For a birth parent the initial loss will usually be felt at or subsequent to the placement of the child. Adoptive parents who are infertile feel a loss in their inability to bear a child. An adopted child may feel a sense of loss at various points in time; the first time the child realizes he is adopted may invoke a strong sense of loss for his birth family.

Mainstreamed

In education, a term that typically refers to the planned and sustained placement of a child with special educational needs into a regular education classroom for part or all of the school day.

Maltreatment

Physical abuse, child neglect, sexual abuse, and emotional abuse. Federal CAPTA legislation (P.L. 104-235) provides definitions that identify a minimum set of acts or behaviors that characterize maltreatment. Each State is responsible for providing its own definitions of child abuse and neglect within the State's civil and criminal context.

Child Abuse and Neglect, according to the Federal legislation, is at a minimum:

- Any recent act or failure to act on the part of a parent or caretaker which results in death, serious physical or emotional harm, sexual abuse or exploitation

- An act or failure to act which presents an imminent risk of serious harm

- Child abuse and neglect typically includes physical as well as emotional abuse (which causes psychological or mental injury), in addition to various types of neglect.

Sexual Abuse is defined in the Federal definition as:

- The employment, use, persuasion, inducement, enticement, or coercion of any child to engage in, or assist any other person to engage in, any sexually explicit conduct or simulation on such conduct for the purpose of producing a visual depiction of such conduct

- The rape, and in cases of caretaker or inter-familial relationships, statutory rape, molestation, prostitution, or other form of sexual exploitation of children, or incest with children.

Matching

The process of finding prospective families specifically suited to meet the needs of a waiting child, not to be confused with "placement".

Maternity home

Residences for pregnant women. The number of homes has decreased over the past three decades, and existing homes often have a waiting list of women. The women who live in a maternity home may pay a small fee or no fee to live in the home and they often apply for public assistance and Medicaid payments.

Mental retardation

Impaired or incomplete mental development characterized by an IQ of 70 or below and characterized by significant functional limitations in at least two of the following skills: communication, self-care, home living, social/interpersonal skills, use of community resources, self-direction, functional academic skills, work, leisure, health, and safety. Onset usually occurs before age 18. More than 200 specific causes of mental retardation have been identified. Degrees of severity reflect the level of intellectual impairment:

- **Mild Mental Retardation**—IQ level 50-55 to approximately 70
- **Moderate Retardation**—IQ level 35-40 to 50-55
- **Severe Mental Retardation**—IQ level 20-25 to 35-40
- **Profound Mental Retardation**—IQ level below 20-25

MEPA

Acronym for Multi-Ethnic Placement Act of 1994.

Multi-Ethnic Placement Act

A federal law enacted in 1994 and implemented through State policy. The Multi-Ethnic Placement Act of 1994, as amended, P.L. 103-382 [42 USC 622] prohibits the delay or denial of any adoption or placement in foster care due to the race, color, or national origin of the child or of the foster or adoptive parents and requires States to provide for diligent recruitment of potential foster and adoptive families who reflect the ethnic and racial diversity of children for whom homes are needed. The 1996 amendment, Section 1808 of P.L. 104-188, Removal of Barriers to Interethnic Adoption, affirms the prohibition against delaying or denying the placement of a child for adoption or foster care on the basis of race, color or national origin of the foster or adoptive parents or of the child involved [42 USC 1996b]

Non-identifying information

Facts about the birth parents or adoptive parents that would not lead to their discovery by another person.

Non-recurring adoption costs

One-time adoption expenses, which may be at least partially reimbursed by States up to a maximum amount to families adopting children with special needs. Allowable expenses for this reimbursement benefit can include the cost of a home study, adoption fees, court costs, attorney fees, physical and psychological examinations, travel to visit with the child prior to the placement, and other expenses related to the legal adoption of a child with special needs.

Occupational therapy

The science of using everyday activities with specific goals, to help people of all ages prevent, lessen, or overcome physical disabilities.

Open adoption

An adoption that involves some amount of initial and/or ongoing contact between birth and adoptive families, ranging from sending letters through the agency, to exchanging names, and/or scheduling visits.

Oppositional defiant disorder (ODD)

A recurrent pattern of negative, defiant, disobedient, and hostile behavior toward authority figures that persists for at least six months. This disorder is characterized by frequent occurrence of at least four of the following behaviors: frequent loss of temper, tendency to argue with adults, refusal to obey adult rules or requests, deliberate behaviors to annoy others, spiteful and vindictive behavior, being touchy or easily annoyed by others, being angry and resentful, use of obscene language, and a tendency to blame others for mistakes or misbehaviors. Symptoms are less severe than those associated with Conduct Disorder but sometimes indicate the early stages of Conduct Disorder (CD) and may sometimes lead to the development of Antisocial Personality Disorder during adulthood.

Orphan

A minor child whose parents have died, have relinquished their parental rights, or whose parental rights have been terminated by a court of jurisdiction.

Orphan (international adoption definition)

For immigration purposes, a child under the age of sixteen years:

- whose parents have died or disappeared or
- who has been abandoned or otherwise separated from both parents or
- whose sole surviving parent is impoverished by local standards and incapable of providing that child with proper care and who has, in writing, irrevocably released the child for emigration and adoption.

To enter the United States, an orphan must have been adopted abroad by a U.S. citizen or be admitted to the to the United States for the purpose of adoption by a U.S. citizen.

Orphanage

Institution that houses children who are orphaned, abandoned, or whose parents are unable to care for them. Orphanages are rarely used in the United States, although they are more frequently used abroad.

Parents patriae

Legal term that defines the State's legal role as the guardian to protect the interests of children who cannot take care of themselves. For example, in an abuse or neglect case, this concept is used to explain the State's duty to protect minor children who lack proper care and custody from their parents.

Passive registries

Type of reunion registry system. Passive reunion registries require both parties to register their consent for release of information before a match can be made. Once a match occurs, both parties are notified. These systems depend on both parties registering, a match being found, and the follow-up notification by a registry administrator.

Paternity testing

Genetic testing that can determine the identity of the biological father. Paternity testing can be done with or without access to the biological mother.

Permanency planning

The systematic process of carrying out (within a brief, time-limited period) a set of goal-directed activities designed to help children live in permanent families. This process has the goal of providing the child continuity of relationships with nurturing parents or caretakers and the opportunity to establish lifetime family relationships.

Photo listing book

A publication that contains photos and descriptions of children who are available for adoption.

Placement date

The time at which the child comes to live with the adopting parents.

Post-institutionalized child

Children adopted from institutional, hospital, or orphanage settings. The term is used to describe an array of emotional and psychological disturbances, developmental delays, learning disabilities, and/or medical problems resulting, in part, from their stay in institutions.

Post-legal adoption services

Services provided subsequent to legal finalization of the adoption. There are primarily four types of post-legal service providers: social service agencies, private therapists, mental health clinics and self-help groups.

Post-placement supervision

The range of counseling and agency services provided to the adopted parents and adopted child subsequent to the child's adoptive placement and before the adoption is legally finalized in court. Social worker reports of this required supervisory period are forwarded to the court.

Post-reunion issues

A range of feelings from euphoria to despair possible after the reunion of birth relatives. Family members in reunion may feel a "let down" or a range of feelings including guilt, anger, jealousy, confusion or happiness that may be related to completion of the reunion process and the beginning of a process whereby family members do or do not negotiate an ongoing relationship.

Post-traumatic stress disorder (PTSD)

A condition in which victims of overwhelming and uncontrollable experiences are subsequently psychologically affected by feelings of intense fear, loss of safety, loss of control, helplessness, and extreme vulnerability and in children the disorder involves disorganized or agitated behavior.

Prenatal substance exposure

Fetal exposure to maternal drug and alcohol use, which can significantly increase the risk for developmental and neurological disabilities. The effects can range from severe (neurological damage and growth retardation) to minor (resulting in normal outcomes). Infant and child long-term development depends not only on the prenatal exposure (type of drug, amount, length of time of use), but on factors related to the child's own biological vulnerability and environmental conditions.

Psychological parent

A person, though perhaps not biologically related to a child, whom the child considers as his parent; sometimes called a "de facto" parent.

Putative

Generally regarded to be true.

Putative Father

Legal term for the alleged or supposed father of a child.

Putative father registries

Registry system that serves to ensure that a birth fathers' rights are protected. Some states require that birth fathers register at these facilities, while other states presume that he does not wish to pursue paternity rights if he doesn't initiate any legal action.

Reactive attachment disorder

A condition with onset before age five, resulting from an early lack of consistent care, characterized by a child's or infant's inability to make appropriate social contact with others. Symptoms may include failure to thrive, developmental delays, failure to make eye contact, feeding disturbances, hypersensitivity to touch and sound, failure to initiate or respond to social interaction, indiscriminate sociability, self-stimulation, and susceptibility to infection.

Relinquishment

Voluntary termination of parental rights; sometimes referred to as a surrender or as making an adoption plan for one's child.

Residential care facility

A structured 24-hour care facility with staff that provide psychological services to help severely troubled children overcome behavioral, emotional, mental, or psychological problems that adversely affect family interaction, school achievement, and peer relationships.

Residential treatment

Therapeutic intervention processes for individuals who cannot or do not function satisfactorily in their own homes. For children and adolescents, residential treatment tends to be the last resort when a child is in danger of hurting himself or others.

Respite care

Temporary or short-term home care of a child provided for pay or on a voluntary basis by adults other than the parents (birth, foster, or adoptive parents).

Reunification

The returning of foster children to the custody of their parent(s) after placement outside the home.

Reunification services

Interventions by social worker and other professionals to help children and their birth parents develop mutually reciprocal relationships that will help them to live together again as a family.

Reunion

A meeting between birth parent(s) and an adopted adult or between an adopted adult and other birth relatives. The adopted adult may have been placed as an infant and thus has no memory of the birth parent(s).

Ritalin

A commonly prescribed drug that can help to control some of the symptoms of attention deficit disorder. It may have a calming effect and help to improve concentration.

Search

An attempt, usually by birth parent, adopted person, or adoptive parent (but sometimes by volunteers or paid consultants) to make a connection between the birth parent and the biological child.

Search and consent procedures

Procedures, sanctioned in State law, that authorize a public or private agency to assist a searching party to locate another party to the adoption to determine if the second party agrees to the release of identifying information or to meeting with the requesting party. If consent is given, the disclosure of information may then be authorized by the court. In some states counseling is required before information is received.

Semi-open adoption

An adoption in which a child's birth parents and pre-adoptive parents may exchange primarily non-identifying information. After the child is placed in the adoptive home, contact with the birth family may involve letters or pictures or other communications sent through the intermediary of the adoption agency or the attorney who assisted in the placement.

Sexual abuse

The employment, use, persuasion, inducement, enticement, or coercion of any child to engage in, or assist any other person to engage in, any sexually explicit conduct or any simulation of such conduct for the purpose of producing any visual depiction of such conduct; or rape, and in cases of caretaker or inter-familial relationships, statutory rape, molestation, prostitution, or other form of sexual exploitation of children, or incest with children.

Sexual abuse symptomology

Indicators and behaviors, which suggest that a child may have been sexually abused, including: excessive masturbation, sexual interaction with peers, sexual aggression towards younger and more naive children, seductive behavior, and promiscuity.

Special needs children

Children whose emotional or physical disorders, age, race, membership in a sibling group, a history of abuse, or other factors contribute to a lengthy stay in foster care. Guidelines for classifying a child as special needs vary by State. Common special needs conditions and diagnoses include: serious medical conditions; emotional and behavioral disorders; history of abuse or neglect; medical or genetic risk due to familial mental illness or parental substance abuse.

Speech and language disorders

Impairments of speech or receptive language. Speech disorders usually involved difficulties with articulation, which can generally be improved or resolved with speech therapy, usually requiring treatment over months or years. Language disorders, on the other hand, often result in substantial learning problems, involving difficulty with language comprehension, expression, word-finding and/or speech discrimination. Treatment by a language therapist generally leads to improvement in functional communication skills, although treatment cannot be generally expected to eradicate the problem.

Stepparent adoption

The adoption of a child by the new spouse of the birth parent.

Substitute care

Any kind of care sanctioned by the court of jurisdiction in which the child does not live with the birth parent.

Supplemental Security Income (SSI)

A Federally funded needs-based disability program for adults and children which provides monthly cash benefits and, in most states, automatic Medicaid eligibility.

Surrender

Voluntary termination of parental rights. An action taken by birth parents to voluntarily "make an adoption plan" for a child or "relinquish": a child for adoption.

Surrender papers

Legal document attesting to the signator's voluntary relinquishment of parental rights to a child.

Surrogate mother

A woman who carries another woman's child by pre-arrangement or by legal contract.

System

Often referred to as "the public child welfare system." Refers to the network of governmental organizations providing a range of child welfare services.

Termination of Parental Rights (TPR)

The legal process, which involuntarily severs a parent's rights to a child.

Therapeutic (or treatment) foster home

A foster home in which the foster parents have received special training to care for a wide variety of children and adolescents, usually those with significant emotional or behavioral problems. Parents in therapeutic foster homes are more closely supervised and assisted more than parents in regular foster homes.

Tourette's syndrome

A treatable neurological disorder that consists of involuntary "tic" movements or vocalizations that become more apparent under stress. Common manifestations include shoulder-shrugging, neck-jerking, facial twitches, coughing, grunting, throat clearing, sniffing, snorting, and barking. Children with Tourette's often have problems with hyperactivity as well.

Traditional adoption

Most often used to refer to a domestic infant adoption in which confidentiality is preserved. Equivalent to a closed adoption.

Treatment Foster Home

A foster home in which the foster parents are trained to offer treatment to children with moderate to severe emotional problems; also known as therapeutic foster home.

Voluntary adoption registry

A reunion registry system which allows adoptees, birth parents, and biological siblings to locate each other if they wish by maintaining a voluntary list of adoptees and birth relatives.

Waiting children

Children in the public child welfare system who cannot return to their birth homes and need permanent, loving families to help them grow up safe and secure.

Glossary reprinted in whole from: http://naic.acf.hhs.gov/admin/glossary.cfm
Administration for Children and Families,
U.S. Department of Health and Human Services
National Adoption Information Clearinghouse
330 C Street, SW
Washington, DC 20447

References

Bogan, J. (2004, January 22). Baby-buying case on border delayed Woman accused of bringing pregnant women to Laredo. *San Antonio Express-News Border Bureau*, p. 1A.

Bogan, 2004

Bogan, J. (2004, May 21). Baby Buyer is heading to prison. *San Antonio Express-News Border Bureau*. Retrieved November 16, 2004, from http://www.mysanantonio.com/news/crime/stories/MYSA052104.1B.bondoc-sentence.e7760c2a.html

Bogan, 2004

Ernst, P., Kushner, L., Adoption Visions, a.k.a. Adoption Visions Family Services L.L.C.,. (2000). [Specific Release and Agreement]. Unpublished raw data.

Adoption Visions, 2000

Goodman, E. (2001, January 26). Twin girls and their cyberspace fate. *The San Diego Union-Tribune*. Retrieved June 11, 2003, from http://www.adoptionnation.com/ellengoodman.html

Goodman, 2001

Hwang, S. (2004, September 28). U.S. Adoptions Get Easier. *The Wall Street Journal*, p. D1.

Hwang, 2004

Johnston, P., & Williams, W. (1997, January). Losing an Adoption: Practical Advice for Moving on after a Uniquely Painful Experience. *Perspective Press' Fact Sheets*. Retrieved May 21, 2003, from http://perspectivespress.com/item.asp?recordid=losingadopt&pagestyle=default

Johnston, Williams, 2003

Kimberly, J. (2002, September 19). Teen's complaint leads to arrests at adoption agency. *Houston Chronicle*. Retrieved July 07, 2003, from http:// houstonchronicle.com/

Kimberly, 2002

McDonald, J. (2003, March 12). Indictment spotlights adopt. *The San Diego Union-Tribune*. Retrieved May 14, 2003, from http://www. signonsandiego.com/news/metro/

McDonald, 2003

National Adoption Information Clearing House, U.S. Department of Health & Human Services Administration for Children & Families. Retrieved June 08, 2004, from http://naic.acf.hhs.gov/admin/glossary.cfm

NAIC, 2004

Pertman, A. (2000). *Adoption Nation How the Adoption Revolution Is Transforming America*. New York: Basic Books.

Pertman, 2000

Roseman, E. (2000). [Rituals and Ceremonies in Celebration of Adoption]. Unpublished raw data.

Roseman, 2000

Roseman, E. (2000). [The Internet Twin Story-Who's To Blame?]. Unpublished raw data.

Roseman, 2000

Roseman, E. (2002, November). Entitlement Issues: Are We The Real Parents? *Cooperative Adoption Consulting*, 1-4.

Roseman, 2002

Ryan, J. E. (2002). *Broken Spirits~Lost Souls Loving Children with Attachment and Bonding Difficulties*. Lincoln: iUniverse, Inc.

Ryan, 2002

Slobodzian, J. A. (2000, September 9). 4-year term in adoption swindle. *The Philadelphia Inquirer*, pp. B1, B4.

Slobodzian, 2000

Stiles, M. R. (2000, April 11). News Release from United States Attorney's Office of Eastern District Pennsylvania. Retrieved April 11, 2000, from http://www.usao-edpa.com/releases/apr/furlow.html

Stiles, 2000

United States Of Am. v. Sonya Furlow, Government's Change of Plea mem.

The E.D. of Pa., 2000

Zarazua, J. (2003, April 17). Mom may sue adoption agency. *San Antonio Express-News Border Bureau*. Retrieved July 30, 2003, from http://news.mysanantonio.com/story.cfm?xla=saen&xlb=180&xlc=981711

Zarazua, 2003

About the Author

Kelly Kiser-Mostrom is from the heartland of Nebraska and the adoptive mother of four children. She has pursued adoptions for twenty years with agencies, attorneys, facilitators, and the Department of Family Services. The impact of these events in her life has compelled her to share those experiences. Adoption holds a special place in her heart as her husband and other family members are also adoptees. Articles relating to *The Cruelest Con* have been reported nationally in *Time Magazine, U.S. News and World Report, 48 Hours* and *Dateline*.

978-0-595-34998-2
0-595-34998-6

Printed in the United States
72102LV00013B/217